The New Americans
Recent Immigration and American Society

Edited by
Steven J. Gold and Rubén G. Rumbaut

A Series from LFB Scholarly

Unequal Origins
Immigrant Selection and the Education of the Second Generation

Cynthia Feliciano

LFB Scholarly Publishing LLC
New York 2006

※ 61864285

Library of Congress Cataloging-in-Publication Data

Feliciano, Cynthia, 1973-
  Unequal origins : immigrant selection and the education of the second
generation / Cynthia Feliciano.
      p. cm. -- (The new Americans)
  Includes bibliographical references and index.
  ISBN 1-59332-087-6 (alk. paper)
  1. Children of immigrants--Education--United States--Cross-cultural
studies. 2. Immigrants--Education--Cross-cultural studies. 3.
Educational attainment--United States--Cross-cultural studies. I. Title.
II. Series: New Americans (LFB Scholarly Publishing LLC).
  LC3746.F45 2006
  371.826'9120973--dc22

2005028676

ISBN 1-59332-087-6

Printed on acid-free 250-year-life paper.

Manufactured in the United States of America.

Contents

Tables and Figures

vii

Acknowledgments

I could not have completed this book without the generous support of many people and institutions. Initial work was funded by fellowships from the Ford Foundation, the Social Science Research Council and UCLA. Vilma Ortiz encouraged me to pursue the "selectivity question" in the initial stages of formulating the project; she also provided constructive feedback throughout the process. Min Zhou's outstanding contributions to the study of children of immigrants provided a strong foundation for the development of my research project. Meredith Phillips and Abel Valenzuela provided careful readings and criticisms of my work. I also owe a special thanks to Rebecca Emigh, Katy Pinto, Tiffani Chin, and participants in the UCLA Sociology department's professional writing class, the SSRC International Migration Program's Minority Summer Workshop, and the Center for Comparative Social Analysis Workshop for their comments and suggestions on several chapters. A University of California President's Postdoctoral Fellowship at the University of California, Irvine greatly facilitated the process of writing the book. I thank Rubén Rumbaut for his mentorship under the fellowship and his guidance in completing the book. I am also grateful to Elizabeth Castellanos and Karen Ivy for their assistance with word processing and editing in the final stages of completing the book.

CHAPTER 1

Introduction

The United States has witnessed a phenomenal rise in immigration over the past few decades. As immigrants settle in the United States, major concerns have centered on how immigrants adapt in their new country. In the long term, however, the key question regarding the impact of recent immigration is how the children of these immigrants are incorporated into U.S. society. Research on the second generation—children of immigrants raised in the United States—has pointed to a striking diversity of outcomes that varies systematically by national-origin, especially in educational attainment, the most important predictor of eventual economic success in the United States.

This book explores how immigration, as an inherently unequal process characterized by differential selection of migrants, contributes to educational inequality among children of immigrants in the United States. I argue that a previously neglected aspect of immigration—its selective nature—helps explain educational disparities among the second generation. Immigrant selection, or selectivity, refers to the fact that immigrants differ in important ways from those who do not migrate. While immigration scholars agree that migrants are not random samples of the populations from which they originate, they disagree about how immigrants compare to persons remaining in their origin countries. In terms of educational attainment, for example, scholars do not agree on whether immigrants tend to be positively selected (more educated relative to nonmigrants in the home country), or negatively selected (less educated than nonmigrants). Further, among those who are positively selected, it is unclear whether immigrants are much more highly educated than their nonmigrant counterparts (high selectivity), or whether their educational advantage is minimal (low selectivity). This book systematically analyzes immigrants' educational selectivity and its effects on second-generation educational inequalities. In doing so, it focuses on structural characteristics of immigrant national-origin groups by determining the segment of the home country's class structure from which immigrants tend to be drawn and the socioeconomic status of the immigrant group once it has settled in the United States. It explores the ways that these immigrant *group* structural characteristics shape the achievement of next generation *individuals* raised in the United States, beyond the influences of their own immediate family members.

In this introductory chapter, I present the research problems I am investigating, provide some background on contemporary immigration to the United States and the new second generation, and provide an overview of the remainder of the book.

Statement of the Problem

Understanding socioeconomic disparities among children of immigrants is particularly important because these disparities may persist across future generations (Borjas 2004, 1994; Glazer and Moynihan 1963; Hirschman and Falcon 1985; Steinberg 1981). The roots of second-generation success and failure may provide the key to why some groups seem stuck in poverty, why others join the mainstream middle class, and why some, like the Jews and Japanese, achieve extraordinary success (Hirschman and Falcon 1985; Treiman and Lee 1996; Waldinger and Lichter 1996). As Min Zhou (2001:301) states, "the central question for today's research remains that of accounting for ethnic differences."

Contemporary second-generation national-origin groups differ markedly in educational outcomes. For example, Asian-origin youths tend to be more academically successful than Latin-American-origin youths. In 2003, 32% of Asian high school graduates in California, having completed the required courses with adequate grades, were eligible to attend the University of California, compared to only 7% of Latinos (California Postsecondary Education Commission 2005). Such group differences persist even after controlling for post-migration family background measures such as parental educational attainment, income, and occupational status. Steinberg and his associates (1996), for example, found that after controlling for family background, ethnic differences persisted in educational achievement, as well as in many beliefs and behaviors related to educational success, such as educational aspirations and time spent on homework (Steinberg 1996; Steinberg, Brown, and Dornbusch 1996). These studies, however, only consider characteristics of immigrant parents in the post-migration context of the United States.

While many explanations have been offered to explain ethnic differences among the second generation (see Chapter Two), the impact of the pre-migration status of the first generation has generally been neglected. Overlooking immigrant selectivity—how immigrants' characteristics compare to those remaining in the country of origin— limits the current literature's understanding of the *observed* patterns of assimilation or socioeconomic mobility of major immigrant groups in the United States. In general, this literature does not ask how the socioeconomic circumstances of immigrants in their origin countries relate to where the second generation becomes situated in the U.S. While recent research on the second generation has problematized the question of assimilation *to what* by pointing out the various ways that immigrants and their offspring adapt once they are in their new country (Portes 2003; Portes and Rumbaut 2001; Portes and Zhou 1993), relatively little immigration research has focused on pre-migration origins (see Rumbaut 1997 for an exception). This neglect is puzzling given the widespread agreement that "origins shape destinies" (Rumbaut 1997: 13). This book problematizes the question of assimilation *from what* by examining how immigrant origins relate to second-generation destinies.

I focus on education for two major reasons. First, educational attainment is a fairly stable outcome in adulthood and data is available for immigrants in the United States as well as from multiple countries. Because of this, education provides a useful benchmark of where immigrants were situated in their home countries' stratification systems prior to migration, as well as how their children are faring in the United States. Second, and perhaps more importantly, education is the major predictor of subsequent economic outcomes, such as earnings or occupational status, in the United States (Blau and Duncan 1967).

Contemporary Immigration to the United States

Immigration is currently transforming American society and, some argue, has a greater demographic impact on the United States now than ever before. Due to tremendous population growth in general, the foreign born[1] actually comprise a smaller percentage than they did at the turn of last century: in 1890, immigrants accounted for nearly 15% of the total U.S. population, while in 2000, they comprised 11% (Figure 1.1). Yet as Figure 1.2 shows, more foreign-born persons currently reside in the United States than at any other time. Specifically, both as a proportion of the total population and in terms of absolute numbers, the rise in immigration over the past 35 years has been remarkable. In 1970, slightly fewer than 10 million immigrants in the United States made up less than 5% of the total population. By 2000, over 30 million immigrants accounted for 11% of the total population. The influence of immigration is especially apparent in schools, since one in five school-age children live in immigrant families (Suárez-Orozco and Suárez-Orozco 1995; Zhou 1997).

Figure 1.1. Percent of U.S. Population who are Foreign-Born, 1890-2000

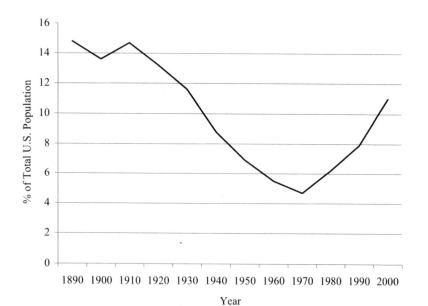

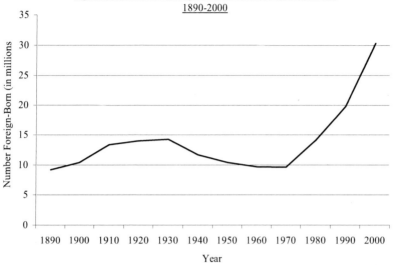

Figure 1.2. Number of Foreign-Born Persons in the United States, 1890-2000

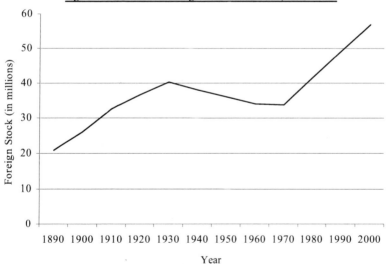

Figure 1.3. Number of Foreign Stock[1] in the U.S., 1890-2000

Figure 1.3 shows that the "foreign stock" of the United States population, which includes immigrants as well as the second generation—those born in the United States with at least one foreign-born parent—numbers over 56 million persons (as of 2000). While Figure 1.4 shows that this group was a larger percentage of the total U.S. population in the early 1900's, it has been steadily growing since 1970. By 2000, one fifth of the total national population was either first or second generation.

Along with the tremendous rise in immigration to the United States over the last few decades, the national origins of U.S. immigrants have also changed dramatically. Figure 1.5 illustrates these changes using INS data on legal immigrants only. As the figure shows, those who migrated at the turn of the century were overwhelmingly from Europe and Canada (nearly 97%). By mid-century, Europeans and Canadians still dominated U.S. immigration, but a growing minority of migrants came from Latin America and Asia. By the 1990's, however, the

Figure 1.4. Foreign Stock as Percentage of U.S. Population, 1890-2000

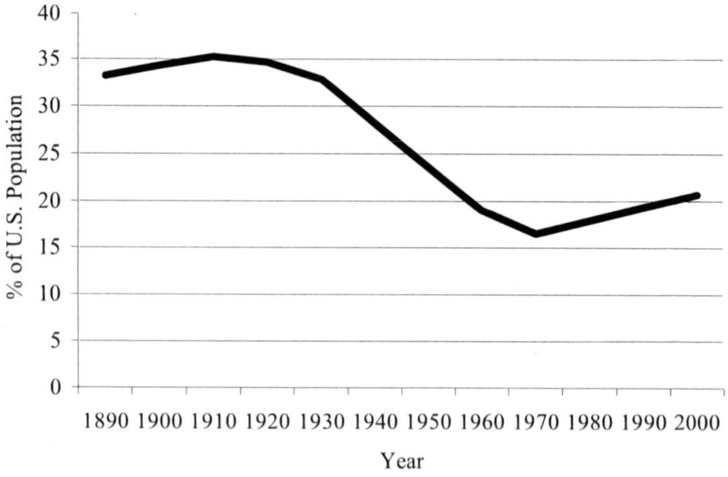

Figure 1.5. The Changing Regional Origins of Legal U.S. Immigrants

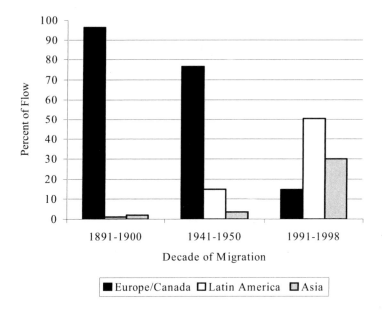

regional mix of migrants had changed substantially. Over half of all legal migrants who arrived in the 1990's were from Latin America, 30% were from Asia, and only about 15% were from Europe or Canada. This shift has led to considerable debate about how the new immigrants and their children will assimilate in comparison to their European forerunners.

The changing national origins of contemporary U.S. immigrants are also reflected in Table 1.1, which shows the approximate number of foreign-born persons from each country, as well as the percentage they hold among the total number of foreign-born persons in the United States. The table includes all national-origin groups with at least 70,000 people residing in the United States in 2000, which includes over 90% of all U.S. immigrants. I have highlighted in bold the 32 national-origin groups that are the focus of the later chapters in the book. Among the top 15 origin countries, five are either European or Canadian

Table 1.1. Foreign Born[1] in the U.S., by Country of Origin and Size, 2000

Country	N	% of FB	Country	N	% of FB
Mexico[2]	**8069532**	**25.42**	Trinidad &	173915	0.55
Philippines	**1313513**	**4.14**	**Portugal**	**173788**	**0.55**
Puerto Rico	**1236677**	**3.90**	Brazil	164157	0.52
Germany	1147104	3.61	Central	160696	0.51
India	**1009950**	**3.18**	**Thailand**	**160645**	**0.51**
Cuba	**957004**	**3.01**	Ukraine	148623	0.47
China	**897810**	**2.83**	Venezuela	140113	0.44
Canada	**879088**	**2.77**	**Greece**	**137577**	**0.43**
Vietnam	**872553**	**2.75**	Asia	132619	0.42
South Korea	**801632**	**2.53**	Lebanon	131401	0.41
El Salvador	**787425**	**2.48**	Egypt	126051	0.40
Dom. Rep.	**698949**	**2.20**	**Yugoslavia**	**122963**	**0.39**
England	636433	2.00	Cambodia	122556	0.39
Italy	**500710**	**1.58**	Turkey	113669	0.36
Poland	**457985**	**1.44**	**Netherlands**	**103749**	**0.33**
Colombia	**439955**	**1.39**	Spain	102268	0.32
Jamaica	**422388**	**1.33**	Romania	99048	0.31
Haiti	**384608**	**1.21**	Scotland	98789	0.31
Russia	**370465**	**1.17**	Israel	94257	0.30
Japan	**357175**	**1.13**	Panama	93293	0.29
Peru	**333819**	**1.05**	Europe	92220	0.29
Taiwan	333382	1.05	Argentina	90849	0.29
Guatemala	**328587**	**1.04**	Nigeria	89288	0.28
Iran	**310514**	**0.98**	Caribbean	87060	0.27
Ecuador	**286438**	**0.90**	**Hungary**	**86872**	**0.27**
Honduras	**254813**	**0.80**	Chile	86475	0.27
Nicaragua	**252318**	**0.79**	Bangladesh	84488	0.27
Ireland	**210400**	**0.66**	Iraq	81356	0.26
Guyana	202653	0.64	South Africa	80418	0.25
Hong Kong	**201437**	**0.63**	Ghana	80082	0.25
Pakistan	196486	0.62	Costa Rica	78247	0.25
France	190161	0.60	Laos	73815	0.23
			Uruguay	72963	0.23

Source: March Current Population Survey, 2000 [1] Foreign born includes those born in outlying areas of the United States. [2] Countries in bold are those studied in this book.

Table 1.2. Second Generation[1] in the U.S., by Country, Size, and Age

Country	N	%	Ave Age	Country	N	%	Ave Age
Mexico[2]	**6762021**	**24.3**	**18.1**	Norway	185285	0.7	66.7
Italy	**2185823**	**7.9**	**58.3**	Sweden	182994	0.7	63.0
Canada	**1672094**	**6.0**	**46.8**	**Guate-mala**	**179369**	**0.6**	**12.5**
Germany	1349839	4.9	40.6	France	167514	0.6	32.0
Puerto Rico	**1297776**	**4.7**	**23.0**	**Nether-lands**	**158390**	**0.6**	**45.7**
Poland	**998998**	**3.6**	**60.6**	**Portugal**	**157985**	**0.6**	**36.3**
England	834781	3.0	45.8	**Hondur-as**	**145091**	**0.5**	**15.4**
Philipp.	**815643**	**2.9**	**19.3**	**Ecuador**	**142942**	**0.5**	**17.8**
Ireland	**618571**	**2.2**	**52.5**	**Yugo-slavia**	**140666**	**0.5**	**50.2**
Russia	**615976**	**2.2**	**68.7**	Taiwan	125024	0.5	12.6
El Salv.	**574134**	**2.1**	**16.1**	**Peru**	**123866**	**0.5**	**12.9**
Dom. Rep.	**513948**	**1.9**	**13.7**	Spain	122756	0.4	39.1
Cuba	**453669**	**1.6**	**19.3**	Pakistan	120336	0.4	5.8
China	**433568**	**1.6**	**24.7**	Guyana	111799	0.4	14.3
India	**346221**	**1.2**	**14.6**	**Iran**	**111115**	**0.4**	**14.0**
S. Korea	**293895**	**1.1**	**13.8**	**Thailand**	**105518**	**0.4**	**11.6**
Hungary	**274657**	**1.0**	**59.8**	Lebanon	101400	0.4	30.4
Greece	**265411**	**1.0**	**37.8**	**Nicar-agua**	**100386**	**0.4**	**20.7**
Japan	**262259**	**0.9**	**40.4**	Cambodia	99781	0.4	12.7
Austria	257232	0.9	63.3	Lithuania	93647	0.3	65.6
Scotland	248304	0.9	52.6	Romania	79175	0.3	49.1
Jamaica	**226591**	**0.8**	**17.8**	**Hong Kong**	**78086**	**0.3**	**14.7**
Haiti	**225132**	**0.8**	**14.7**	Denmark	76422	0.3	60.9
Vietnam	**219318**	**0.8**	**9.0**	Ukraine	75684	0.3	51.9
Czech.	200579	0.7	63.2	Turkey	74842	0.3	40.4
Colomb.	**188217**	**0.7**	**14.6**	Trinidad & Tobago	71805	0.3	13.2

Source: March Current Population Survey, 2000. [1]The 2nd Generation includes those born in the 50 states, with at least one parent born outside the 50 states. [2] Countries in bold are those studied in the book.

(Germany, Canada, England, Italy, Poland), five are Latin American (Mexico, Puerto Rico[2], Cuba, El Salvador, Dominican Republic), and five are Asian (Philippines, India, China, Vietnam, South Korea). Mexicans dominate contemporary migration flows: over one-quarter of all foreign-born individuals in the United States were born in Mexico, amounting to over eight million people. No other country even comes close in terms of numbers, although the Philippines, Puerto Rico, Germany and India have each sent over one million people to the United States.

Table 1.2 shows estimates of the second generation[3] in the United States in 2000, by group size and average age. Again, all other groups are dwarfed in comparison to the Mexican second generation who, with over 6 million persons, accounts for over 24% of the second generation in the United States. However, sizable numbers of U.S.-born children of immigrants from European countries, most notably Italy, Germany, Poland, and England, also live in the United States. From their average ages, it is obvious that the current second generation is made up of children of immigrants from vastly different periods of migration. With the exceptions of those from Greece, Portugal, and France, all of the second-generation Europeans are over 40 years old on average, including many groups who average nearly 60 years or older (Italians, Poles, Russians, Hungarians, Austrians, Czechoslovakians, Norwegians, Swedish, Lithuanians, and Danish).

In contrast, the Japanese are the only Asian second-generation group to have an average age above 40 (40.4). In fact, many Asian groups are such recent migrants that most of their second generations are still children. For example, the average age of the Indian and South Korean second generations are less than 15 years old, while the Vietnamese second generation is only 9 years old, on average.

Likewise, the young average ages among the second generation from Latin America or the Caribbean also reflect relatively recent migration flows. The Puerto Rican and Nicaraguan second generations, for example, are the only Latin American/Caribbean groups to average (barely) over 20 years old in 2000.

Because of their sheer numbers, contemporary immigrants and their children will certainly impact U.S. society in crucial ways. To further understand how immigrants' children will incorporate into U.S. society, and what their impact will be, it is important to look at characteristics of the immigrant generation. Table 1.3 compares the distribution of educational attainment among immigrants to U.S. natives, showing that immigrants tend to be less educated than their native counterparts. For instance, 11% of the foreign born above age 25 have attended some high school, but did not graduate. This percentage drops to 9% when looking at the U.S.-born population. In addition, over 21% of immigrants did not attend high school at all, compared to less than five percent of U.S. natives. Nonetheless, sizable proportions of the foreign born are represented at the top of the educational distribution as well. In fact, a similar proportion of the foreign born and the U.S. born have graduated from college or received graduate degrees. The story of the immigrant generation, therefore, is one of educational polarization, with substantial percentages of immigrants at both the bottom and the top of the educational distribution.

Table 1.3. Educational Attainment of Immigrants and Natives in the United States, ages 25+

	U.S.-born	Foreign-born
less than high school	4.55	21.54
some high school	8.63	10.88
high school graduate	34.5	24.96
some college	26.75	16.96
college graduate	17.17	16.19
graduate/professional degree	8.42	9.46

Source: March Current Population Survey, 2000

Table 1.4 shows how immigrants' socioeconomic diversity varies by country of origin, by presenting the percent with less than a high school education, percent college educated, and poverty rates. As is typically the case, educational attainment and poverty are negatively correlated. For example, Mexicans, Puerto Ricans, and Dominicans not only have the highest poverty rates, but are also the least likely to have high school or college degrees. Socioeconomic disparities between some of the groups, such as Indians and Mexicans, are striking. Consequently, national-origin disparities in the adaptation of the second generation may not seem surprising. Nor would it be surprising if status attainment processes that operate among children of U.S. natives replicated themselves among immigrants' children—with parents' education and occupation, as measured in the United States, largely accounting for educational differences. However, numerous studies have found strong effects of ethnicity (or national origin) on the educational achievement or attainment of the second generation, even after controlling for parents' post-migration education, income, and occupational status (Portes and Rumbaut 2001; Rumbaut 1997). How to account for these persistent educational disparities is a major puzzle motivating this book.

Table 1.4. Educational Attainment and Poverty Rates for Foreign-Born[1] Adults, ages 25+, in the United States, by Country of Origin, 2000

Country	% poor	% less than hs educated	% college educated
Mexico	21.95	65.37	4.33
Philippines	5.20	13.15	43.72
Puerto Rico	22.11	46.00	12.00
Germany	6.23	7.18	36.12
India	8.04	9.22	72.68
Cuba	18.32	30.04	21.32
China	11.27	20.45	43.53
Canada	7.41	12.95	35.23
Vietnam	16.45	30.87	19.30
South Korea	8.43	10.05	43.32
El Salvador	13.28	65.34	3.91
Dominican Republic	29.93	51.84	8.59

[1] Foreign born includes those born in Puerto Rico.

Overview of the Book

The chapters to follow emphasize the importance of characteristics of immigrant groups in shaping educational outcomes among the second generation. Building upon prior research showing that individual *and* contextual factors shape divergent outcomes, I chart the connection between variations in immigrant group selectivity and educational outcomes among the second generation. I link structural and cultural explanations for ethnic group differences by arguing that a structural characteristic—immigrant groups' educational selectivity—shapes cultural expectations and aspirations for educational success, which ultimately determine educational attainment. I use data from multiple sources, including U.S. Census data, Current Population Survey data, Census data from immigrant-sending countries (gathered from United Nations Educational, Scientific, and Cultural Organization), and Children of Immigrants' Longitudinal Survey data.

Chapter Two presents a theoretical overview of the literature on second-generation incorporation and explanations for ethnic group differences in educational outcomes. I present the segmented assimilation framework, which I build upon throughout the study, and discuss cultural and structural explanations for variations in school performance. I conclude the chapter with a discussion of the literature on immigrant selectivity and how it may be linked to second-generation outcomes.

Chapter Three, "Those Who Stay and Those Who Leave," adjudicates the selection debate itself in a critique of scholars who argue that immigrant selectivity affects socioeconomic outcomes, but who only use proxies for selectivity in their empirical work. Since examining selectivity's effects requires comparable data on both the sending and receiving sides of the migration process, I compile a unique dataset from published educational attainment statistics in 32 of the top immigrant-sending countries to the United States, and census data on U.S. immigrants from those countries. My findings run contrary to the common assumption that many immigrants are negatively selected, coming from low socioeconomic positions in their home countries.

In fact, nearly all immigrants (with the critical exception of Puerto Ricans) are positively selected, or more educated than the populations in their home countries. Asian immigrants are more highly selected relative to their home country populations than Latin American immigrants, and there is some evidence that earlier waves of Mexican immigrants are more positively selected than later waves. My findings challenge theoretical frameworks based on case studies of Puerto Rico by showing that the finding that Puerto Rican migrants are less educated than their homeland population cannot be generalized to any other immigrant group, all of whom face much greater barriers to entry to the United States. I also find evidence contrary to the argument that immigrants are less skilled than in the past by showing that more recent immigrants (mainly from Latin America and Asia) actually tend to be more highly selected than those who arrived in the 1960's (mostly from Europe).

Chapter Four, "Immigrant Origins and Second-Generation Ambitions," explores the mechanisms through which immigrant selectivity shapes educational aspirations and expectations among second-generation youths. I analyze data from the Children of Immigrants Longitudinal Survey (1992-1996), merged with the immigrant selectivity measures calculated in Chapter Three. The analyses control for a rich array of family background factors, including parents' post-migration socioeconomic status. The findings show that parents from highly selective immigrant groups have higher aspirations, which lead to greater educational expectations and aspirations among their children. Furthermore, even when these parents do not have robust aspirations, youths' educational expectations remain high. The results underscore the interaction effects between group and individual-level factors. The effect of parents' post-migration socioeconomic status on students' educational expectations depends upon the selectivity of the immigrant group to which they belong. That is, if the immigrant group as a whole is highly selective, the children will have high educational expectations even if their parents are struggling economically. The analyses suggest that group selectivity matters partly for cultural reasons, in that higher group selectivity generates higher educational expectations.

Chapter Five, "Immigrant Origins and Second-Generation Attainment," shifts the focus to the educational attainments of adult children of immigrants. I examine whether differences in the degree of immigrants' educational selectivity influence educational attainment outcomes among groups of immigrants' children using the data gathered in Chapter Three, as well as data on children of immigrants from the 1990 Census and 1997-2001 Current Population Surveys. I show that as the relative level of education attained by immigrants in their home countries increases, the educational attainment of the second generation, in terms of average years of schooling, high school graduation rates, and college attendance rates, does also. Moreover, the fact that a higher percentage of Asian immigrants are among the better-educated of their home population than immigrants from other countries helps explain their second generations' higher college attendance and high school graduation rates as compared to Europeans, Afro-Caribbeans, and Latinos. The findings suggest that some national-origin groups excel in school while others lag behind because inequalities in relative pre-migration educational attainments among immigrants are often reproduced among their children in the United States.

Chapter Six discusses the implications of immigrant selectivity for the actual observed assimilation and mobility patterns of various immigrant groups. That is, relative to their parents' pre-migration status, is the second generation experiencing upward or downward mobility in the United States? I show that a consideration of the starting point used for assimilation trajectories matters tremendously. For example, Mexicans, Salvadorans, and Dominicans may be viewed alternately as experiencing upward or downward mobility relative to their parents depending upon whether we consider the initial reference point to be pre- or post-migration. I argue that not only is the pre-migration socioeconomic position a stronger predictor, but it also takes into account that the meaning of education varies depending on the context in which it is undertaken. Along these lines, I show that among groups to whom substantial upward mobility is attributed, some were actually of relatively high status prior to migration, and others, such as Mexicans, Salvadorans, and Dominicans, are in fact experiencing downward mobility when compared to the pre-migration status of the immigrant generation.

Finally, Chapter Seven concludes the book with a summary of the main findings, implications of the study, and directions for future research.

NOTES

[1] In this figure, persons born in outlying areas of the U.S. are classified as natives, as are persons born in a foreign country, but with at least one parent who was a U.S. citizen.

[2] Although Puerto Rico is part of the United States, the same processes are involved in the migration of Puerto Ricans to the mainland United States as for immigrants from other countries. For this reason, I include Puerto Ricans as immigrants throughout this book. Puerto Rican migration is different from international migration, however, in that Puerto Ricans do not face legal barriers to entry. In subsequent chapters, I argue that this fact leads to divergent findings.

[3] I define the second generation as those born in the 50 states, with at least one parent born outside the United States or in Puerto Rico. I base the country of origin on the father's place of birth, unless the father was born in the United States, in which case I base the country of origin on the mother's place of birth.

CHAPTER 2

Explaining Ethnic Differences:
Cultural and Structural Views

Much of the literature has suggested that differences in educational attainment among the second generation are rooted in characteristics of the immigrant generation. However, previous literature has been hindered by an artificial "culture" versus "structure" dichotomy. Researchers argue that the primary determinants of educational differences among immigrants' children are *either* culturally situated "values" *or* structurally defined class background. I argue that this divide is too simplistic, and that both are actually closely intertwined. Differences in educational characteristics among immigrant adults have structural components, in terms of knowledge and skills made available to children, and cultural components, in terms of the motivations, expectations, and aspirations passed on. Existing research has not adequately measured such intertwined factors since it has largely focused on absolute measures of socioeconomic status (such as absolute levels of educational attainment or occupational status in the United States) or speculated about values (in the absence of actually measuring them). I offer an alternative approach to explaining differences in educational success among the second generation that considers the role of the educational selectivity of the adult immigrant generation. Educational selectivity (the difference between the immigrants' educational attainment and the average educational attainment in their homeland) captures not only skill level, as absolute educational attainment does, but relative pre-migration status, which may influence the expectations of different groups regarding where their children belong in the U.S. stratification system.

In addition, I argue that differences among the immigrant generation and the second generation should be analyzed at the group level of analysis in addition to the individual level. Differences in immigrants' skills and motivations not only affect their children, but also the entire group's educational trajectory for at least two reasons. First, perceptions about groups have meaningful consequences. Thus, if a group is considered a "model minority," this perception will positively benefit all the children of immigrants in that group, even if a particular immigrant family does not fit the stereotypical image. Second, ethnic groups and communities are important resources beyond the family, and the skills and motivations of group members determine the strength of immigrant communities. Therefore, second-generation youths from relatively low status families may nevertheless benefit from belonging to a high status ethnic group.

This chapter provides a review of the literature on immigration and second-generation adaptation. In particular, I present an overview of segmented assimilation theory, a framework I draw upon to situate the findings throughout this book. I also engage the debate between cultural and structural explanations for ethnic group differences in socioeconomic success. I then promote a serious consideration of the influences that group-level characteristics and processes have on individual socioeconomic outcomes. I conclude the chapter with a discussion of immigrant selectivity and how it may relate to second-generation success.

Segmented Assimilation and Second-Generation Adaptation

While straight-line assimilation theory predicted a single trajectory of upward mobility over time and across generations in the United States (Gordon 1964; Park 1928), the reality never exactly matched the theory, even among earlier waves of migration from Europe. The straight-line view implied that the path is the same for all groups, but empirical evidence has shown that different European groups progressed at divergent rates with vast differences in educational and occupational attainments among the second generation, even controlling for post-migration family background factors (Perlmann 1988; Thernstrom 1973). Nevertheless, some contemporary scholars argue that the straight-line model of slow upward mobility fits the experience of most groups, and new immigrant groups are not that different from their turn of the century European counterparts (Alba and Nee 1997; Perlmann and Waldinger 1997).

In contrast to the straight-line view, the segmented assimilation framework adds two more possibilities for immigrant adaptation (Portes and Zhou 1993; Portes and Rumbaut 2001). In addition to a gradual upward mobility across generations, an immigrant group may also achieve rapid economic advancement within a strong ethnic community by using ethnic group membership as a source of beneficial social capital (Coleman 1988; Portes and Zhou 1993; Zhou and Bankston 1998). A third alternative is that an immigrant group remains in permanent poverty or experiences downward integration if immigrants' children fail to graduate high school or go on to college (Gans 1992; Portes and Zhou 1993; Zhou 1997). As it is the most troubling, this third path of downward assimilation has received the bulk of attention in scholarly debates (Perlmann and Waldinger 1997; Waldinger and Feliciano 2004). The possibility of "second-generation decline" means that children of immigrants who fail to graduate from high school or go on to college are at risk of creating a new a multiethnic "rainbow underclass" by joining the blacks and native-born Hispanics who are currently shut out of the mainstream economy (Gans 1992; Portes 2003).

The segmented assimilation view emphasizes the role of both individual and contextual factors, and the interactions among them, offering a framework for understanding why different ethnic groups incorporate into U.S. society in divergent ways (Zhou 1999). In doing so, this literature argues that the experiences of contemporary immigrants' children differ from those of European immigrants' children. There are several reasons why this might be the case. First, economic restructuring in the United States has resulted in an "hourglass economy" characterized by many jobs at the high or low extremes, and few jobs in the middle (Gans 1992; Portes and Zhou 1993). This has led to a decline in the number of well paying blue collar jobs, which, some argue, were important mobility ladders for some immigrant groups in the past (Portes and Zhou 1993; Vernez 1997). The result is that higher education has become an increasingly important criterion for advancement. However, many children of recent immigrants are concentrated in the inner city, where poverty, poor schools, decreasing job opportunities, and the lure of drugs and violence make it unlikely that many will go to college (Portes and Zhou

1993; Zhou 1997). Gans (1992) argues that children of immigrants who grow up in the United States, and thus lack a direct comparison to their homeland, will not accept the menial, service-oriented "immigrant" jobs of their parents, if these jobs are even offered to them. Therefore, the absence of stable blue collar jobs could mean that if children of immigrants fail to graduate from high school or go on to college, they risk greater poverty than their parents. In addition, the new immigrant children, unlike European immigrants of the past, are visibly identifiable as not white.[1] Some argue that the prejudice and discrimination they face is therefore decidedly worse than that encountered by European immigrants and their children, and may substantially limit their life chances or the mechanisms available to them to be upwardly mobile (Gans 1992; Portes and Zhou 1993).

In contrast to the straight-line assimilation view that suggests that time in the United States should lead to more positive socioeconomic outcomes, recent scholarship sees a stronger pattern of second-generation decline. Several studies have shown that longer U.S. residence leads to worse educational outcomes for a number of different groups (Gibson 1988; Kao and Tienda 1995; Matute-Bianchi 1991; Rumbaut 1997; Rumbaut 1999; Sewell and Hauser 1980; Suárez-Orozco and Suárez-Orozco 1995; Vernez and Abrahamse 1996). Regardless of the influence of acculturation, however, the most striking differences in educational outcomes remain *between* ethnic groups (Feliciano 2001; Kao and Tienda 1995; Portes and Macleod 1996; Rumbaut 1997; Steinberg, Brown and Dornbusch 1996). Even statistical analyses that control for a rich array of post-migration background factors show persistent ethnic group differences in academic achievement and aspirations (see, e.g. Portes and Rumbaut 2001; Rumbaut 1999). Explaining these between-group differences remains the most vexing question surrounding the adaptation of the second generation (Zhou 2001).

Cultural and Structural Explanations for Group Differences

Understanding the causes of ethnic differences in socioeconomic outcomes is a long-standing and fundamental sociological problem. In the United States, racial and ethnic differences in educational attainment and achievement in particular have persisted throughout this century. On most measures of educational success, Asians rank highest followed by whites, with blacks and most Latino groups lagging behind.[2] For example, high school graduation rates exceed 90% for Asians and whites, but are only about 80% for blacks and Latinos (Mare 1995). While the achievement test scores of black and Latino students rose during the 1970's and 1980's, blacks and Latinos still score, on average, well below their Asian and white counterparts (Jencks and Phillips 1998; Mare 1995). Black and Latino high school graduates are less likely to go to college than Asians or whites, and blacks and Latinos who do enroll in college are less likely to graduate (Mare 1995). Educational attainment patterns among children of immigrants appear to follow the existing trends of racial/ethnic differences in the United States. Most Asian subgroups' educational successes surpass those of Latin American or Caribbean subgroups. Even children of poorer immigrants, such as Vietnamese and Sikh Indians, have much higher average educational attainments than similarly impoverished groups, such as Mexicans or Salvadorans (Feliciano 2001; Gibson 1988). Sociological explanations for socioeconomic differences among ethnic and racial groups in the United States consist of two main strands of thought: cultural theories and structural perspectives. The first emphasizes the role of cultural factors, such as values, beliefs, and attitudes, in explaining group differences. The second emphasizes the role of structural factors, such as class background and the opportunity structure.

One of the main structural explanations for why Latinos and blacks do worse in school than their Asian or white counterparts concerns differences in family background. The influential and controversial Coleman Report (1966) found that family background factors, including socioeconomic status and family structure, were the most important factors explaining black-white differences in achievement test scores (Coleman et al. 1966). Differences in family socioeconomic status, including parents' education, income and occupation, have been shown to explain about 1/3 of the black-white test score gap and to explain much of the difference in a host of other educational outcomes (Hedges and Nowell 1998; Herrnstein and Murray 1994).

Stratification research has shown how socioeconomic background is converted into socioeconomic status through schooling, aspirations, and parental encouragement (Hauser and Featherman 1977; Sewell, Haller and Portes 1969). These works suggest that socioeconomic outcomes depend not just on family origins, but also on a number of (unmeasured) individual factors, such as luck (Jencks et al. 1972). However, this perspective fails to fully explain racial or ethnic differences in socioeconomic outcomes, and ignores constraints and processes that operate beyond the individual level to affect the group.

The real puzzle is to explain why, controlling for socioeconomic background in the United States, blacks and Latinos have lower achievement rates in school than whites and Asians. Part of the answer may be that typical measures of "class," such as parents' education, income, and occupational status, do not capture other differences that are crucial. Phillips et al (1998) find that controlling for additional socioeconomic factors, such as grandparents' educational attainment and parenting practices, can explain up to 2/3 of the black-white test score gap. Similarly, Banks (1988) argues that traditional measures of class status alone cannot explain why middle class whites outperform middle class blacks. He contends that we must also look at "generational middle class status" (Banks 1988). White youths are more likely to have grandparents who also have similarly high levels of education as their parents. On the other hand, middle class black parents are much more likely to have been upwardly mobile and to have come from working class backgrounds. For the children in these families, this may mean that radically different social resources are available within each family. The white family is more likely to see high educational attainment as the norm; the black family may see it as something they *hope* will persist into the next generation.

The white family's middle class status is also likely to be accompanied by more valuable social contacts than that of a black or Latino family. Middle class standing may therefore be more securely transmitted to the next generation for whites. Indeed, Portes and Wilson (1976) show that parental status is much more important in influencing the educational attainment of whites than blacks. While Mare (1995) argues that "secular improvements in minority educational status imply that each successive generation of minority parents improves its average level of educational attainment" (209), this view assumes that black and Latino parents automatically transmit their educational standing to their children. If, however, that transmission depends not just on parents, but other characteristics of their social groups, the story may not be this straightforward.

When class and family background do not appear to fully explain group differences, many scholars have turned to cultural arguments.

These arguments have often been invoked, in particular, to explain national-origin differences in socioeconomic outcomes among early 20th century European immigrants' children, specifically those between "model minority" Jews and lesser achieving Italians. Today, scholars pose similar arguments to explain the success of "model minority" Asian newcomers, such as the Vietnamese and Chinese, as compared to the lesser achieving Latino newcomers, such as those from Mexico, the Dominican Republic, and Central America.

To explain Jewish educational success, many scholars have emphasized a reverence for learning rooted in the homeland. For example, by showing how important education was to the lives of Shetl Jews in their home country, Zborowski and Herzog (1962) imply that Jews carried this value of education with them to the United States and passed it on to their children. Similarly, Glazer and Moynihan (1963) focus on the Jewish "passion for education" and devotion to learning (Glazer and Moynihan 1963). Gordon (1964) argues that the rapid socioeconomic mobility of Jews, despite the fact that they started at "the bottom," can be attributed to their having "arrived in America with middle-class values already internalized" (Gordon 1964: 187). Even Perlmann (1988) (who also discusses the importance of structural factors) implies that there is an independent effect of Jewish culture on their socioeconomic success. He contends that because religious scholars in traditional Jewish culture were highly respected and visible, Jewish immigrants valued learning in general (Perlmann 1988).

Such cultural arguments ignore the structural advantages of the Jews and how those advantages influenced their values. The Jews, unlike many other immigrants arriving at the turn of the Century, were not peasants (Goldscheider and Zuckerman 1984; Perlmann 1988; Steinberg 1981). While most Jewish immigrants were indeed poor, the majority was literate and came with skills acquired from their experiences in urban commerce (Goldscheider and Zuckerman 1984; Perlmann 1988; Steinberg 1981). While these structural differences distinguished Jews from other immigrant groups, it is also likely that Jews were positively self-selected compared to those who remained behind in their countries of origin. However, these studies only control for immigrants' socioeconomic background in the United States.

The Jewish case is often juxtaposed against that of the Italians. While the gap in socioeconomic status between Italians and other European immigrant groups is negligible today,[3] data from East Coast cities in the earlier half of the 20th century reveal lower rates of school enrollment and graduation for Italian-American children than for children of other white ethnic groups (Covello and Cordasco 1967; Perlmann 1988). Many scholars also invoke cultural arguments to explain Italians' lower educational achievement. Covello (1967) argues that Southern Italian peasants' indifference towards education was passed on to their U.S.-born children, accounting for the low educational attainment of Italian-Americans. Similarly, Glazer and Moynihan (1963) argue that the main factor inhibiting the progress of second-generation Italian-Americans was the negative attitude towards school of Southern Italian parents, who came from villages where "intellectual curiosity and originality were ridiculed" (199). Like Covello, they conclude decisively that "the burden of Southern Italian culture" held back the progress of Italian Americans (Glazer and Moynihan 1963: 201). Gans (1982), examining the Italian-American community in Boston's West End, implies that the public school was at odds with the Italian family's tendency to be "person-oriented," and thus primarily concerned with good behavior and discipline rather than educational achievement. Likewise, Glazer and Moynihan (1963) contend that Italians value family advancement more than individual achievement in school.

These arguments, however, ignore the structural conditions that create attitudes, values and behaviors. Even if the homeland culture is the prime influence on attitudes towards education among Italians in the United States, as Covello (1967) argues, that culture is itself probably a response to structural conditions in Southern Italy. The central government neglected to fund educational facilities in that region, and the agricultural economy depended on children's labor. Likewise, the problematic relationship of Italian immigrants and their children to schooling was, above all, a response to structural constraints in the United States. Perlmann (1988) notes that parents were not opposed to school; however, their class situation made investments in their children's education irrational and unnecessary. Unlike Jews, Italians had peasant backgrounds, were largely illiterate, and had few marketable skills (Perlmann 1988). Given these circumstances, a child's contribution to the family income was often more essential to the immediate well being of the family than their schooling. Still, even controlling for family class background, Italian-American children lagged behind other groups in school success (Perlmann 1988). A possible explanation is that standard family background measures (such as parents' education and occupational status) do not capture the degree to which Italians were less selective than other immigrants.

Today, the unresolved Jewish/Italian debate is being replayed with a new set of actors from Asia and Latin America. Asians, like Jews, are frequently thought of as a "model minority." They have enjoyed extraordinary socioeconomic success in a relatively short period of time, particularly within the educational sphere. On average, native-born Asians enjoy the highest educational attainment levels of all the broad ethnic groups in the United States, including native-born whites (Cheng and Yang 1996). Of course, Asians are from diverse backgrounds, and are actually composed of about 25 nationalities. While not all of these groups have been overwhelmingly successful, the educational attainment of many of these groups, such as the Chinese, Japanese, and Asian Indians, has been remarkable.

Reminiscent of the Jewish case, many arguments suggest that the unique cultural characteristics of Asians explain their achievements in education. Sowell (1981) attributes the success of Japanese immigrants to the high value they place on reading and education. Others emphasize the "fit" between the value systems in Asian countries and American middle class values (Caudill and DeVos 1956; Hirschman and Wong 1986). Some contend that the Confucian culture's reverence for learning drives Asian parents to push their children to do well in school (Cheng and Yang 1996). Still others argue that Asian success is rooted in their family values, and that their stable family life provides an environment that is conducive to children's success in school (Cheng and Yang 1996).

However, as Steinberg (1981) points out, attributing Asian success to "values" makes little sense when one is lumping together groups from 25 or so different countries, each with its own unique cultural traditions. It seems that scholars tend to assume a common culture based on similar rates of success. However, as Steinberg (1981) notes, there are some Asian groups, such as Cambodians, that are not nearly as successful as others. Cultural explanations would seem to imply that these groups are somehow deficient in "Asian" values (Steinberg 1981).

Cultural arguments ignore the importance of pre-migration characteristics and the ethnic community's resources in explaining Asian success. The history of Asian exclusion may have actually made

Chinese and Japanese immigration very selective (Cheng and Yang 1996; Hirschman and Wong 1986). In contrast to immigrants such as Mexicans, who have a longer, less restricted history of migration to the United States, most Asian migrants do not have family ties in the United States that they could draw upon to gain entry to the United States. Therefore, most Asian immigrants tend to be quite selective since until recently, they could only immigrate under the 1965 Immigration Act's skilled worker provisions. Indeed, Cheng and Yang (1996) found that foreign-born Chinese, Japanese, Korean, and Asian Indians are more educated than even native-born whites. It is therefore quite likely that the comparison to those left behind in the homeland is even more extreme, and that these immigrants are more highly selected than their counterparts from other countries. It is not necessary to invoke notions of homeland cultural values to explain Asian success in education. More sophisticated arguments recognize how cultural characteristics interact with structural conditions to lead to Asian success. For example, Sue and Okazaki (1990) argue that cultural values combined with limited opportunities in areas other than education lead Asians to focus their effort and motivation into school achievement (Sue and Okazaki 1990). Zhou and Bankston (1998) link cultural values to structure by emphasizing how social relations within ethnic communities serve as control mechanisms that allow values to be reinforced. However, the selective immigration of high status Asians may be what accounts for those educational values and what allows for the creation of strong ethnic communities.

Group-level Characteristics and Processes

Recent scholarship on the second generation has suggested that it is necessary to move beyond individual-level determinants to understand diverse ethnic group outcomes. The segmented assimilation theory, for example, emphasizes that factors external to a particular group, such as the racial hierarchy and economic structure, as well as group characteristics, such as financial and human capital, community organization, and social relationships, are important determinants of second-generation adaptation (Zhou 1999).

Part of the reason individual-level factors are not enough to explain group differences is that groups are perceived differently, and group reputations shape individual perceptions of self and others. While all non-white national-origin groups face some type of discrimination in the United States, the meanings attributed to membership in different racial categories vary greatly. For example, employers rank different groups in terms of desirability (Lieberson 1980; Waldinger 1996). While there certainly has been racism directed towards Asians, it is also true that "model minority" stereotypes, especially concerning educational abilities and work ethics, are overwhelmingly positive. Positive stereotypes of Asian-Americans can lead to a "halo effect" that may help even the children of the newest Asian groups, such as the Vietnamese, who often come from less advantageous class backgrounds, succeed in school (Zhou and Bankston 1998). The "halo effect" creates positive expectations in teachers or in students themselves, which may become self-fulfilling prophecies.

Borjas's (1992) analysis of "ethnic capital" shows empirically how group-level characteristics shape individual achievement. Defining "ethnic capital" as the average skill level in the father's generation, Borjas (1992) shows how this group characteristic influences the next generation's skills above and beyond parental capital. Building upon Coleman's (1988) concept of social capital, Borjas (1992: 126) argues that the average "quality" of the ethnic environment in which a child is raised exposes that child to "social, cultural, and economic factors that influence their productivity when they grow up."

Portes and Rumbaut (1996) also argue that persistent national-origin differences in attainment, controlling for individual-level background factors, suggest that "broader cultural or social factors" affect collective group performance. The concept of group "modes of incorporation" is useful to understand group differences (Portes and Borocz 1989; Portes and MacLeod 1996; Portes and Rumbaut 1996). Modes of incorporation are affected by (1) governmental policies, such as whether the immigrants are given resettlement assistance, as many refugees are, or whether they are denied legal entry; (2) societal reception, such as prejudice and discrimination; and (3) the strength of ethnic communities, including social networks and resources. Thus, it is not only parents who are important, but rather, "the entire weight of the experiences of an immigrant group plays a key role in its children's education" (Portes and MacLeod 1996: 392).

While understanding divergent modes of societal incorporation is necessary in an analysis of group adaptation, the concept tends to emphasize factors within the United States while paying less attention to how the migration process itself produces diverse groups prior to arrival in the new country. The strengths and weaknesses different immigrant groups confront stem both from the "contexts of reception" they face in the United States, as well as the "contexts of exit" from their countries of origin (Rumbaut 1997). As Portes and Borocz (1989) point out, existing theories are inadequate to explain why migration occurs from and to particular countries or why only certain individuals within each country migrate. To understand these processes, a complex analysis of the historical relationship between sending and receiving countries, as well as the social networks that propel migration, is necessary (see Massey 1986, 1987b). While such an analysis is beyond the scope of this book, I do explore outcomes of that complex process—selective immigration—through an examination of the segments of different home country populations that come to the United States.

The Selectivity Question

As Rumbaut (1999: 187) writes, "origins shape destinies." Indeed, current immigration scholarship has noted the diverse class character of contemporary immigration in terms of the occupational and educational composition of migrants from different countries (see, for example: Bean and Stevens 2003; Rumbaut 1996, 1997, 1999). Such absolute measures of socioeconomic status, however, do not come close to fully capturing the origins of contemporary immigration flows. They tell us little about the context within which occupations and educations were attained, and thus how the origins of immigrants from different countries compare to each other. After all, most recent immigrants to the United States come from developing countries, but what is remarkable is that many immigrants, especially from poorer countries in Asia, are not themselves poor or uneducated (Rumbaut 1996, 1997). Depending on the educational and occupational structure in the country of origin, immigrants with the same educational or occupational credentials from one country may have had much higher status than those from another country. Further, while most studies only control for immigrants' socioeconomic status in the United States, many groups experience downward mobility after migration due to language and adjustment difficulties. Understanding relative pre-migration status—

captured by selectivity—might tell us more about different groups' expectations for the next generation's status attainment.

Immigrants' selection, or who comes and who does not come to the United States, occurs in a number of ways. For instance, immigrants may self-select (relative to those in the home country who do not wish to migrate or do not have the resources to do so), or be selected by U.S. immigration and refugee policies (relative to those who would like to migrate to the United States but cannot do so legally) (Rumbaut 1999). Some argue that all immigrants, whether legal or illegal, represent a select group from the home country (Portes and Rumbaut 1996; Treiman et al 1986), while others argue that only some immigrants are positively self-selected (Borjas 1987, 1990b). In either case, it is likely that positive selectivity is greater for immigrants from some countries than from others. In other words, even if Mexican immigrants are more highly educated, on average, than the norm for Mexico, the degree to which their education is higher than average may not be as great as that of immigrants from other countries, such as the Philippines.

In general, the topic of immigrant selectivity is under researched (Gans 2000), and its full exploration is beyond the scope of this book. However, I do begin to answer the question of how immigrants compare educationally to those who do not migrate, and how this selection varies by country of origin. Further, this book explores how such differences in immigrant selection influence educational outcomes among the next generation. Although this influence has been suggested by previous research, it has not been explicitly examined. For example, ample literature shows that in the case of the Vietnamese and Punjabi Sikhs, second-generation youths excel in school beyond what is expected for their socioeconomic background (Gibson 1988; Zhou and Bankston 1998). Kao and Tienda (1995) find that children of immigrants perform better in school than their third generation counterparts within the same panethnic group. They argue that this is accounted for by their parents' optimistic outlook about opportunities in the United States, which compels the youths to be more achievement driven. This optimistic outlook may itself be a product of the circumstances producing migration and the selectivity of immigrants (Kao and Tienda 1995). If migrants are self-selected to adapt to their new country, they may expect that their children will experience upward mobility (Chiswick 1978; Borjas 1990a; Ogbu 1991). This book will test this hypothesis by explicitly evaluating the selectivity of migrants and its impact on second-generation educational outcomes.

Summary

In this chapter I have reviewed some of the existing theoretical perspectives guiding the study of second-generation educational adaptation and proposed ways in which it may be related to group-level processes such as immigrant selectivity of the first generation.

Segmented assimilation theory is one of the principal perspectives that guides this study. The innovation in segmented assimilation theory is its specification of divergent paths and outcomes of immigrant adaptation, rather than the single trajectory suggested by classic assimilation theories. The segmented assimilation framework emphasizes the influence of both individual and contextual factors, but cannot clearly account for persistent ethnic group differences in educational achievement among second-generation immigrant groups (Zhou 2001). Solutions to the long-standing sociological problem of how to account for ethnic differences in socioeconomic outcomes have been hindered by an artificial division of culture vs. structure. I argue that structural differences, such as from which segment of the socioeconomic structure immigrants are drawn, may influence the cultural expectations that are passed on to the next generation. Structure and culture are intimately intertwined.

The segmented assimilation view suggests that the characteristics of entire immigrant groups, rather than those of just families or parents, influence the next generation's educational trajectories. I argue that the question of immigrant selectivity—how those who migrate to the United States compare to those who are left behind in origin countries—is important because differences in immigrant selectivity may capture differences in group-level resources that affect the adaptation of the second generation.

NOTES

[1] Many European immigrants were "racialized" at the turn of the century. However, physical differences are greater among contemporary immigrant groups and, for that reason, many scholars expect the perception of racial differences to persist.

[2] This literature review discusses differences among four broad groups: Asians, whites, blacks, and Latinos. The subsequent chapters in the book also focus on these groups. However, I only study children of immigrants. While the theories in this literature can be applied to explain ethnic differences among children of immigrants, the reader should keep in mind that "blacks" in the literature usually refers to African-Americans—descendants of slaves—while the "blacks" in my study are children of recent West Indian immigrants.

[3] Of course, extensive intermarriage has made such comparisons less meaningful than they used to be. Most who identify as Italian today are actually of mixed European ancestry. Also, it is quite possible that Italians would still lag behind other European groups if they had not intermarried.

CHAPTER 3

Those Who Stay and Those Who Leave

Surprisingly, current immigration research has not adequately addressed the basic question of how immigrants' characteristics compare to those who remain in the sending society (Gans 2000). The seemingly simple fact that migrants are not random samples of their home countries' populations has long been uncontested (Borjas 1987, 1999; Lee 1966; Ravenstein 1885). Beyond this, however, little is known about immigrant selectivity or the patterns and determinants of the selection process.

In particular, immigrants' educational selectivity—how educated immigrants are relative to those remaining in the country of origin—is important for two main reasons. First, the characteristics of those who leave a country may dramatically affect the remaining population. In developing countries, "brain drain," or the out-migration of highly educated professionals, may hinder future progress and development by depriving the population of major resources such as leadership and occupational skills (Glaser 1978; Grubel and Scott 1977; Vas-Zoltan 1976). Second, educational selectivity may affect how well immigrants and their children adapt in the United States. The characteristics of immigrants (e.g., the education, wealth, and skills they bring with them) clearly affect their economic integration in the U.S. (Portes and Rumbaut 1996: chap. 3). However, few studies consider the effects of immigrants' pre-migration characteristics, such as where they were situated in the educational distribution of their origin country.

Understanding the educational selection of immigrants may shed light on why some immigrants and their descendents are more successful in the United States than others, and why these ethnic differences persist for many generations (Borjas 1999: chap. 3). Hirschman and Falcon (1985), for instance, found that the low educational attainments among some groups of immigrants generally continue in successive generations. Parental schooling, they concluded, is the most important factor explaining educational differences across groups, and has both cultural as well as economic consequences (Hirschman and Falcon 1985). Because educational opportunities differ substantially by country, immigrants who do not have high educational credentials by American standards may, in fact, be quite selective relative to the general populations in their home countries (Lieberson 1980: 214). Therefore, immigrant parents' relative pre-migration education may influence their children's educational outcomes as much as their formal level of schooling in the U.S. context. In addition, educational selectivity differences may be associated with resource disparities among immigrant groups, affecting various socioeconomic outcomes for both immigrants and their children (Treiman et al. 1986). For instance, highly selective immigrants may have greater economic resources, such as business skills, than other immigrants; they may also have greater cultural resources, such as higher educational expectations for their children.

Theories of Immigrant Selectivity

In addition to education, various characteristics such as occupation, skills, age, ambition, and gender also influence the immigration process. Selectivity for all of these characteristics occurs on several complex and interrelated levels. First, immigrants self-select: only some people wish to migrate and have the resources to do so. Second, immigrants are selected by legal strictures: some countries, such as China, the former Soviet Union, and the Dominican Republic, have had restrictive exit policies allowing only certain individuals to emigrate (Foner 2000). Third, immigrant flow is influenced by political and economic conditions in the sending country (Massey 1999; Menjivar 1993; Rumbaut 1997). Fourth, labor demands affect selectivity of economic migrants from different countries (Massey 1999). Fifth, the historical relationship between the United States and sending countries guides immigrant selection (Rumbaut 1995; Rumbaut 1997). Finally, immigrants, at least legal ones, are selected by U.S. immigration policy (Green 1999; Lobo and Salvo 1998a, 1998b; Rumbaut 1999). While a full investigation of these selection processes is beyond the scope of this book, I would like to shed light on one outcome concerning how immigrants compare educationally to those in their origin countries.

Scholars who speculate about the answer to this question have disagreed considerably. The early view, expressed as far back as the 1700's by Benjamin Franklin (1753, quoted in Abbott 1969:415-16), who maintained that the Germans were "the most stupid of their own nation," was that immigrants were the poorest of the poor, coming to the United States to escape desperate poverty and unemployment (see also Portes and Rumbaut 1996). This view, which is still espoused in the popular press by those who denounce immigration, is even found in some contemporary scholarly writings (Briggs 1975; Lamm and Imhoff 1985; Teitelbaum 1980).

However, this belief has largely been replaced by newer debates. Some researchers now argue that all immigrants, whether legal or illegal, represent a positively select group from the home country because they are more ambitious and willing to work, or have higher levels of education than their counterparts who stayed behind (Portes and Rumbaut 1996: chap 1; Treiman and Lee 1996). Chiswick (1978) used the idea that immigrants are highly self-selected to explain why immigrants do so well in the labor force, particularly compared to natives. Portes and Rumbaut (1996: 12-13) argue that migrants are the most ambitious and motivated of their home countries, but have no means to fulfill their aspirations without leaving. Relative, not absolute, deprivation is what motivates individuals to migrate (Stark and Bloom 1985). Thus, poor and uneducated persons, who are often socially isolated and unaware of migration possibilities, are less likely to migrate than those who are urban, have some education, or have been exposed to the United States' lifestyles (Portes and Rumbaut 1996: 12-13). Indeed, some studies have shown that the very poor and unemployed seldom migrate, legally or illegally (Bean, Browning and Frisbie 1985; Bray 1984; Massey 1987a; Portes 1979). Contrary to popular perception, then, even undocumented immigrants may be positively selected. Since resources are needed to migrate illegally—to pay the costs of hiring smugglers or obtaining fake documents—undocumented migrants may in some cases be more positively selected than authorized immigrants who can be sponsored by relatives in the United States (Bray 1984). This scholarship suggests that immigrants will always be more educated than the general populations remaining in their homelands.

However, in a theoretical discussion of both internal and international migration, Lee (1966) contends that only some migrant streams are positively selected, while others are negatively selected. He argues that the causes of migration are crucial: if migrants are leaving because of "plus factors" in the destination (or pull factors), they will be positively selected. If they are responding to "minus factors" in the sending society (or push factors), they will be negatively selected. Obstacles are also an important factor: immigrants who face the greatest barriers in migrating will be the most positively selected (Lee 1966; Schultz 1984).

Borjas (1987, 1991) also argues that only some immigrants are positively self-selected. Expanding upon Roy's (1951) model of the impact of self-selection in occupational choice on income distributions, Borjas specifies under what conditions immigrants will be positively or negatively selected. He theorizes that immigrants to the U.S. are positively selected only if sending countries have relatively egalitarian income distributions (Borjas 1987, 1991). If the home country's income distribution is more unequal than in the United States, immigrants will be negatively selected, and will come from the lower end of that country's socioeconomic distribution. Thus, Borjas (1987, 1991) argues that skilled Mexicans do not migrate to the U.S. since their skills are more rewarded under Mexico's more unequal system. Unskilled Mexicans are most likely to migrate because they are the most relatively disadvantaged in Mexico. Some studies do suggest that undocumented migrants from Mexico are negatively selected based on education (Borjas 1992b, 1996; Massey and Espana 1987; Taylor 1986, 1987). However, in contrast, Chiswick (2000) argues that a more unequal source country "does not necessarily imply negative selectivity but rather only less favorable positive selectivity" (67). In other words, Chiswick does not expect, as Borjas does, that immigrants from inegalitarian countries will be less skilled or educated than their nonmigrant home country counterparts, but only that they will be less positively selected than immigrants from more egalitarian countries.

Because place of origin data is readily available for migration within the United States, most studies testing theories deal with domestic migrants. This literature, mostly on Southern blacks' migration to the North, shows that migrants tend to be more educated than those staying in the place of origin (Lieberson 1980; Shryock and Nam 1965; Suval and Hamilton 1965; Tolnay 1998). Long-distance migrants within the mainland United States are especially likely to be highly selected by education (Long 1973). However, several studies comparing the characteristics of Puerto Rican migrants to those remaining on the island show more complicated patterns of selectivity (Landale 1994; Landale, Oropesa and Gorman 2000; Melendez 1994; Ortiz 1986; Ramos 1992). For example, Landale, Oropesa, and Gorman (2000) find that children of recent Puerto Rican migrants have lower infant mortality risks than children of nonmigrant Puerto Ricans, suggesting that they are positively selected on characteristics related to infant health. Studies of education have found that Puerto Rican migrants to the U.S. mainland have about the same education or less as their counterparts who remain on the island (Ortiz 1986; Ramos 1992). However, since Puerto Rican and other internal migrants are United States citizens, it is difficult to know whether such findings generalize to other groups.

The existing internal and international migration literature suggests that the degree to which immigrants differ in education level from nonmigrants in their homelands will vary by source country. Even if immigrants are all positively selected, there may be substantial variability in the *level* of selectivity by origin country, such that immigrants from some countries are more positively selected than others. Further, these theories suggest some measurable factors that are related to the degree of selection. Migrants from more educated countries have a greater probability of being less positively selected, since the average schooling level is already relatively high. In addition, these theories suggest that given the greater costs of migrating long distances, people from countries further from the United States should be more highly selected. Another implication stems both from Lee's (1966) theory that migrants responding to push factors will be less selective, and from economists who conclude that selectivity only applies to economic migrants (Chiswick 2000). Thus, political refugees who are responding to push factors may not be as highly selected as others. Finally, according to Borjas (1987), migrants from countries with greater income inequality will be negatively selected, or at least less positively selected, than those from more egalitarian countries.

Selectivity is also related to scholarly debates about skill levels of recent immigrants. Borjas (1999: chap. 3) argues that today's immigrants from developing countries in Asia and Latin America are less skilled than immigrants who came from advanced industrial societies in Europe decades earlier. Conversely, other scholars suggest that immigrants from developing countries are not necessarily less skilled. Rumbaut (1997) argues that simply because immigrants come from less developed countries does not mean that they themselves are drawn from the less educated or skilled segments of those societies. Chiswick (1986) suggests that U.S. policy favoring skill has resulted in an increase in highly selected immigrants from Asia, but this is offset by U.S. policy favoring kinship, which has resulted in an influx of less skilled and less selective immigrants as well. Thus, the changes in the regional origins of migrants in recent decades may not correspond to declining skill levels as Borjas suggests. While selectivity and skills are not necessarily the same, they are highly correlated. Consequently, examining whether the changing national origins of immigrants are associated with a decline in educational selectivity will shed light on whether new immigrants are less skilled than older immigrants.

Massey (1987b, 1999) argues that while migrants tend to be positively selected initially, they become less highly selected over time, as successive waves migrate from a particular country. Social capital is a major force perpetuating migration; for example, having an older sibling who migrated to the United States triples the likelihood of migration among Mexicans (Palloni et al. 2001). With each new act of migration, networks expand, such that more nonmigrants come to know someone who has migrated to the United States (Massey and Espinosa 1997). Over time, as it continues to be driven by social networks, migration becomes less costly, and persons who are not relatively well educated or skilled begin to join the flow (Massey 1987b, 1999; Massey et al. 1993). Tolnay's (1998) finding that the educational selectivity of Southern black migrants to the North has declined over the last 100 years is consistent with this idea. In the case of international migration, U.S. immigration policies based on family reunification further increase the possibility that individuals are able to draw upon social networks to migrate. Prior research based on Mexican Migration Project data finds that Mexican migrants are declining in educational selectivity over time (Durand, Massey and Zenteno 2001). However, the Mexican Migration Project data are not representative of all Mexican immigrants in the U.S. Using more representative data from the Mexican and U.S. Censuses, I will examine whether successive waves of immigrants from Mexico are indeed less educated relative to Mexican nonmigrants than those who immigrated earlier.

Conceptual and Measurement Issues

As mentioned earlier, immigrant selection occurs along a number of different characteristics, some of which are measurable, such as education, and others which are not as easily measured, such as ambition, motivation, and work ethic. Although these unmeasured attributes are related to conditions in the sending country and may also affect immigrants' adaptation in the United States, examining them is beyond the scope of this book. Instead, selectivity is measured in terms of education only, and is conceptualized as differences between immigrants and the home country populations from which they are drawn. To illustrate this, Figure 3.1 compares the percentage of immigrants who have some college schooling or higher with their home country populations for the 32 immigrant groups in this study. As is immediately apparent, immigrants are not randomly drawn from their home country's populations and instead almost always have much more schooling than their nonmigrant counterparts. This difference, between the immigrants' educational attainment and that of the nonmigrants in the home country, is the conceptualization of educational selectivity used in this book.

The operationalization of this selectivity concept necessarily involves measurements relative to the population at the place of origin. However, empirical research has not tested different theories on immigrant selectivity adequately because, due to the difficulty of securing data from multiple countries, most comparative studies of international migration do not include data on nonmigrants, and instead use proxies. For example, based on theories of the factors predicting immigrant selectivity, many researchers have used readily available measures as proxies for selectivity, which even they admit are "ad hoc," such as GDP, income inequality, and distance from the United States (Borjas 1987; Cobb-Clark 1993; Jasso and Rosenzweig 1986). Other researchers have used immigrants' pre-migration

Figure 3.1.Percentage with Some College Schooling or More, Immigrants and Nonmigrants from 32 Countries

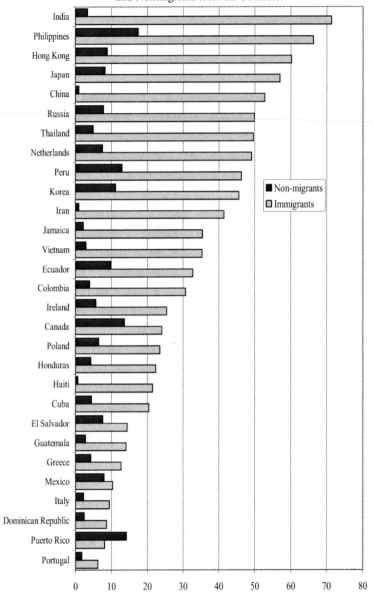

occupational status or absolute level of educational attainment as a proxy for immigrant selectivity (see, for example, Lobo and Salvo 1998b, Rumbaut 1997). Using the formal level of educational attainment as a proxy for selectivity, for example, is problematic because it assumes that a high school degree in one context (say, a country where only 10% of the population earns one), has the same meaning as a high school degree earned in another context (say, where 80% of the population earns one). Thus, including information about those who remain in the homeland is critical to understanding immigrant selection.

Research Questions and Analytic Strategy

This study directly examines the educational selectivity of multiple immigrant groups by comparing immigrants' educational profiles to those of persons in their home countries, using data on *both* the sending and receiving sides of the migration process. In doing so, this chapter addresses several questions. (1) How do immigrants' educational attainments compare to those of nonmigrants in their home countries and how does this vary by country of origin? To answer this question, I calculate a measure of selectivity for multiple immigrant groups, based on comparisons of their educational distributions to those of comparably aged persons in their home countries. (2) How do home country characteristics, reasons for migration, and distance from the U.S. affect immigrant selectivity? Building upon the findings from question one, I use the selectivity measure as an outcome, and analyze whether these country-level factors significantly predict educational selectivity. (3) Are immigrants from regions with more recent migrant streams (Asia/Latin America) more or less educated than those from European countries who migrated in the past? Here, I compare the selectivity of recent migrants from Asia and Latin America to that of older immigrant groups from Europe. (4) Does the selectivity of successive waves of migrants from the same country change over time? This analysis focuses on one national-origin group (Mexicans), and compares different migrant streams from that country at different points in time.

DATA AND METHODS

Data

To compare the educational attainment of migrants and nonmigrants from the same country, age group, and time period, I needed data on immigrants in the United States containing their educational attainment, age, year of immigration, and country of origin. I also needed data on the populations of the major immigrant-sending countries to the United States, including their educational attainment levels, by age, from around the same time period when most immigrants migrated. To assess whether the changing national origin mix is related to changes in immigrant selectivity, I needed data on older immigrant groups from Europe who migrated in previous decades and their nonmigrant counterparts, as well as more recent immigrant groups from Asia, Latin America, and the Caribbean. I also needed data on immigrants and nonmigrants over time from one country with a long migration history to the United States, such as Mexico.

First, I gathered published data on the sending countries' average levels of educational attainment. I searched for data from the top 38 migrant-sending countries to the United States, and ended up with acceptable data (for the appropriate years for that country, by age) from 31 countries and Puerto Rico.[1] The appendix shows the data collected from these countries. Most of the country of origin data were available through UNESCO (United Nations Educational, Scientific, and Cultural Organization) publications. The UNESCO publications compile census data from the various countries and present it in comparable ways. It accounts for the different educational systems in each country by compiling data in six educational categories that are comparable across nations. For Puerto Rico, I used data published by the U.S. Census. I chose the closest year (for which data were available) to the average year of immigration of the U.S. immigrants from that country (calculated from the 1990 Census).[2]

To summarize educational attainment on the receiving side of migration, I created extracts of Census data on U.S. immigrants from each of the 32 countries from the IPUMS (Integrated Public Use Micro Samples). The appendix also summarizes the data on the immigrants used to calculate each immigrant group's educational attainment. Three main principles guided my selection of immigrants for each country's sample. First, since I wanted measures of educational attainment that would reflect those of the "average" immigrant from that country, I included only those immigrants who migrated within 10 years (before or after) the average year a particular immigrant group migrated to the United States. I collected data from the IPUMS for the closest year available following the average years of immigration for that particular national-origin group. In most cases, this meant I used IPUMS data from two decades. For example, if the average year of immigration for immigrants from a certain country was 1980-81, I selected immigrants from that country who migrated from 1975-80 using IPUMS data from 1980, and I selected immigrants from that country who migrated from 1980-86 using IPUMS data from 1990.[3] Second, I limited the sample of immigrants to only those who migrated as adults. Thus, I analyzed data from those who were at least 22 years old when they migrated, so that I could be reasonably sure that most of their education occurred in their home country rather than in the United States. Third, I selected immigrants within the same age range as the home country populations in the published UNESCO data (this is also shown in the appendix).

I then created a small dataset for each immigrant group at the individual-level unit of analysis. I recoded these data on immigrants to match the educational attainment variables that were available through the UNESCO publications for the countries of origin. Thus, I created an educational attainment variable for the immigrants that matched the six educational categories in the UNESCO data on the sending countries: "no schooling/illiterate," "first level incomplete," "first level completed," "second level 1st cycle," "second level, 2nd cycle," and "post-secondary schooling or higher."

For the analyses of changes in immigrant selection among migrants from Mexico, I supplemented the published UNESCO data in 1980 with data from the Integrated Public Use Microdata Series (IPUMS) International samples of Mexican Census data from 1960, 1970, 1990, 2000 (IPUMS for 1980 is not available), and the U.S. Census from 1960-2000. Each is a nationally representative, 1% population sample.[4] The IPUMS international samples are ideal for analyses of trends over time and comparisons between countries because the variables have been recoded to allow for consistency across time and place. I combined the Mexican and U.S. census samples from 1960-2000 to create a dataset for each year consisting of a large sample of Mexicans in Mexico and Mexican immigrants in the United States.

To summarize, I collected educational attainment data on the sending and receiving sides of the migration process for each national-origin group. I collected data on immigrants and nonmigrants from one time period, whenever the migration was most frequent: in some cases this was in the 1960's, in others the 1990's. I also used data on Mexicans and Mexican immigrants from 1960-2000, so I could assess changes over time among immigrants from a single country.

Measuring Educational Selectivity

Before comparing immigrants' educational attainment to that of homeland nonmigrants, I accounted for the differing age distributions of the two populations by using direct age standardization.[5] This standardization is important because immigrants are selected by age as well as education, and because age and educational attainment are related. In most cases, immigrants tend to be younger than those who remain in the homeland. Since most populations are becoming more educated over time, younger adults are generally more educated than older people from the same country. Therefore, not accounting for the differing age distributions would overestimate the degree of positive selectivity, simply because immigrants tend to be younger than nonmigrants. Thus, I re-calculated the educational distributions of the home country populations based on the age structure of the corresponding immigrant group.

Once I consolidated the appropriate age standardized educational attainment distributions, I defined and calculated the selectivity measure—a comparative measure of immigrants' and nonmigrants' educational attainment—to be used in the analysis. While the percentage difference of immigrants and nonmigrants with college schooling compared in Figure 3.1 might be used as one measure of selectivity, it would be too limited. Instead, the measurement of selectivity should compare the overall educational distributions of immigrants and nonmigrants, rather than crude comparisons of mean or median educational attainment or those based on any particular point on the distribution, such as college only. I thus follow Lieberson (1976, 1980), in employing the net difference index (NDI) as the measure of educational selectivity, which is based on the immigrants and the nonmigrants' distributions along all points of the educational range (Lieberson 1976, 1980).[6] The net difference index is based on the percentage of immigrants with the same level of attainment as nonmigrants, the percentage of immigrants with more education than nonmigrants, and the percentage of immigrants with less education than nonmigrants.[7] For example, an index of .35 indicates that an immigrant's educational attainment will exceed that of a nonmigrant from the same country 35% more often than a nonmigrant's education will exceed that of an immigrant from that country (Lieberson 1980). If all immigrants exceed all nonmigrants, the index will be one. If the number of immigrants exceeding nonmigrants in educational attainment equals the number of nonmigrants exceeding immigrants in education, the value of NDI will be zero. Thus, the higher the NDI value, the more educated the immigrants are relative to the nonmigrant population in their home country. If immigrants are more often *less* educated than nonmigrants (that is, if there is negative selection), the value of the NDI will be negative. I calculated the net difference index for both male and female immigrants from each country, as well as separately by gender, where the data were available.

Additional Variables

For my analysis, the primary dataset contains the 32 countries as the units of analysis, the NDI as the measure of educational selectivity, and the original educational attainment variables used to create the selectivity measure. In addition to these measures, I added several additional measures to the dataset. Using U.S. Census data, I calculated, for each country of origin group, the percent who migrated before 1965, the percent of the immigrants who are female, and the average age of the immigrants. Based on the country of origin data, I calculated the average years of schooling in each home country. I also added a dummy variable to distinguish political migrants from others.[8] I added a variable indicating the distance, in thousands of miles, of each country from the United States.[9] Finally, I added the gini coefficient for each country of origin, which is a measure of the degree of income inequality around the time when most immigrants arrived in the United States.[10]

Table 3.1. Educational Selectivity (NDI) of U.S. Immigrants by Country of Origin

Country of Origin	Net Difference Index (NDI)	Net Difference Index, Females	Net Difference Index, Males
Puerto Rico	-0.064	-0.075	-0.050
Mexico	0.200	0.252	0.158
Portugal	0.244	0.265	0.222
Italy	0.260	0.233	0.285
El Salvador	0.342	0.365	0.322
Greece	0.402	0.373	0.426
Cuba	0.406	0.484	0.292
Honduras	0.433	0.447	0.416
Canada	0.434	0.415	0.456
Dominican Republic	0.490	N/A*	N/A
Yugoslavia	0.502	0.511	0.493
Ecuador	0.513	0.537	0.491
Russia	0.520	0.488	0.558
Korea	0.524	0.537	0.505
Hong Kong	0.525	0.472	0.578
Guatemala	0.534	0.560	0.511
Ireland	0.572	0.542	0.617
Poland	0.573	0.605	0.540
Vietnam	0.589	0.545	0.631
Philippines	0.602	0.584	0.631
Colombia	0.617	0.606	0.630
Thailand	0.638	0.594	0.723
Peru	0.645	N/A	N/A
China	0.667	0.662	0.673
Nicaragua	0.669	N/A	N/A
Jamaica	0.670	0.649	0.693
Japan	0.670	0.631	0.722
Netherlands	0.676	0.675	0.677
Haiti	0.710	0.746	0.677
India	0.858	0.640	0.980
Hungary	0.880	0.907	0.859
Iran	0.884	0.875	0.890

* Note: N/A indicates that country of origin data was not available by gender

FINDINGS

How Are Immigrants Selected by Education?

Table 3.1 summarizes the variation in educational selectivity by country of origin for all immigrants, as well as for females and males separately. Focusing on the first column, which presents the net difference index for both male and female immigrants, groups are sorted from the least selective (Puerto Ricans, who are negatively selected: -.064) to the most positively selected (Iranians: .884). The table shows that, with the exception of Puerto Ricans, immigrants from all major sending countries tend to be more educated than the general populations in their home countries. This finding challenges the view that immigrants are the least desirable of their country or that immigrants are only positively selected under certain conditions. This finding is consistent with theories about relative, rather than absolute, deprivation being the motivation for migration, and with observations that it takes a tremendous amount of resources, skills, motivation, initiative, and ambition to emigrate. The finding that immigrants are nearly all positively selected is also true for political refugees, even though their decision to migrate often involves less "choice." Migrants from Iran, Cuba, Vietnam, Russia and Poland (as well as those from countries such as Guatemala and El Salvador who are not granted asylum in the U.S., yet still may flee for political reasons), are all more highly educated than their counterparts who remain in the home country. These findings challenge Lee's (1966) theory that migrants responding to push factors will be negatively selected, at least as applied to international migration.

Puerto Rican migrants are the only exception to the pattern of positive selectivity: the population in Puerto Rico is more highly educated than those who migrate to the United States mainland. The finding that Puerto Ricans are the *only* migrant group that is negatively selected is important for a number of reasons. Puerto Ricans are unique because they are U.S. citizens; therefore, other than the cost of a plane ticket, they face virtually no barriers to entry to the United States mainland. This finding is also consistent with several other studies on Puerto Rican selectivity that found that Puerto Rican migrants are of similar or lower socioeconomic level than nonmigrants (Melendez 1994; Ortiz 1986; Ramos 1992). However, findings from Puerto Rican case studies should not be generalized to immigrants from other countries. Ramos (1992), for example, uses the findings that Puerto Ricans are negatively selected as support for Borjas's theory that immigrants from home countries with highly unequal income distributions will come from the lower end of the socioeconomic distribution. But the theory may only apply in cases where there are no major barriers to entry, such as financial costs, distance, or immigration status. My findings suggest that Borjas's theory is not applicable to most of the major immigrant-sending countries.

The findings also show that, even though all immigrant groups are positively selected, the degree of positive selectivity varies considerably by country of origin. Immigrants from Asia tend to be more positively selected than those from Latin America or the Caribbean. That is, the NDI for eight out of the 13 immigrant groups from Latin America or the Caribbean (Puerto Rico, Mexico, El Salvador, Cuba, Honduras, Dominican Republic, Ecuador, Guatemala) is below the overall median of .553 for the 32 groups, while only two of the nine immigrant groups from Asia has an NDI slightly below the median (Korea, Hong Kong). The variability in educational selectivity by country is striking. For example, Mexican immigrants are more educated than Mexican nonmigrants 20% more often than Mexican nonmigrants are more educated than immigrants (NDI=.200). In contrast, Indian immigrants will have higher educational attainments than Indian nonmigrants 86% more often than the converse is true (NDI=.858).

The second and third columns of Table 3.1 reveal that, while educational selectivity often differs between male and female immigrants from the same country, those differences are generally not great. For example, among the most highly selective immigrant group, Iranians, the NDI for Iranian female immigrants is .890 compared to .875 for men. Likewise, the net difference indexes for Puerto Rican male and female immigrants were similarly low (-.075 for women, -.050 for men). Indeed, the net difference indexes for male and female immigrants were highly correlated (.89). Further, gender differences in educational selectivity do not appear to follow any clear pattern. In over half of the cases, women are less positively selected than men, but women from a substantial minority of the countries are more highly selected than men (12 out of 29 countries). In some cases, the gender differences are much more pronounced than others, with the most noticeable difference between Indian males (.980) and females (.640). Few patterns can be discerned from these gender differences, however. For example, gender differences in educational selectivity are not related to the percentage of immigrants who are female (results available from the author upon request). The only factor that is somewhat related is distance: gender differences in selectivity tend to be greater among immigrants from countries further away from the United States, with these females tending to be less selective than their male counterparts. One possible explanation for this may be that female migrants from distant countries are less likely to migrate for their own job opportunities, but rather to accompany highly skilled husbands who are responding to particular employment opportunities in the United States. Future research is needed to understand these patterns. However, because gender differences in educational selectivity are not substantial, the remainder of the chapter focuses on the overall level of educational selectivity for both male and female immigrants.

Factors Related to Immigrants' Educational Selectivity

Factors such as the relationship between the sending country and the United States, the contexts of exit, U.S. immigration policy, and economic conditions in the sending and receiving country will likely affect the selection of immigrants from any particular country. Narrowing from this general investigation of all such dynamics, I specifically consider in this chapter several possible determinants of immigrant selection that can be straightforwardly operationalized. Possible factors influencing the selectivity of any given group of immigrants that I am able to analyze include the average years of schooling in the home country, the distance of the home country from the United States, the average year of migration, the level of income inequality in the home country, and percentage of those who left for political reasons. I also consider whether the differing age or gender compositions across immigrant groups influence educational selectivity.

Table 3.2 shows correlations between the included variables and immigrant selectivity (NDI), bivariate regression coefficients for NDI regressed on each variable, and multivariate regression coefficients for a model including all significant bivariate relationships. The table

Table 3.2. Relationships between Select Factors and Immigrants'
Educational Selectivity (Net Difference Indexes).

Factors	Correlation Coefficient	Bivariate Regression Coefficient	Multivariate Regression Coefficient
Average Years of Schooling in Home Country	-0.353	-0.041*	-0.043*
Distance (in thousands of miles) from U.S.	0.421	0.029*	0.030*
Percent Who Migrated Before 1965	-0.123	-0.001	
Gini Coefficient (inequality level in home country)	-0.302	-0.007	
Political reasons for migration (dummy variable, 1 if political)	0.240	0.107	
Average age of immigrants	-0.098	-0.004	
Percent of immigrants who are female	-0.087	-0.358	
Constant for multivariate model:			0.665***
R2 for multivariate model:			0.308
N for multivariate model:			32

*p<.05; **p<.01; ***p<.001

shows that the average years of schooling in the home population is
negatively correlated with selectivity (-.353), and that this relationship
is significant: immigrants from highly educated populations are less
likely to be as highly positively selected as those from less educated
populations. Greater distance from the United States is associated with
greater positive selectivity (.421, .029). The negative correlation for the

percent of immigrants migrating before 1965 (-.123) suggests that immigrants from countries that only recently began migrating to the United States tend to be more positively selected than those who came primarily in the 1960's or 1970's. However, this relationship is not statistically significant in the bivariate model. Thus, these findings challenge the popular perception that immigrant skills have declined as the regional origins of immigrants have changed over time. There is a negative association (-.302) between home country inequality and positive selectivity. While this provides some support for Borjas's and Chiswick's claims that immigrants from more egalitarian countries will be more positively selected, income inequality is not a statistically significant predictor of selectivity in the bivariate model. This finding contradicts the theory that immigrants from highly unequal societies are less likely to be positively selected. Further, although there is a positive relationship between political reasons for migration and positive selectivity (.240), it also is not significant. This finding conflicts with the economic view, which assumes that only economic migrants are positively selected. Finally, the correlations show that the average age and the percentage of females in the immigrant group are both negatively correlated with the level of selectivity; however, neither variable significantly predicts educational selectivity. These insignificant results are important because they suggest that the selectivity results are not biased by the different age and gender compositions across immigrant groups.[11]

The multivariate model includes only the significant bivariate predictors of selectivity, average years of schooling in the home country and distance from the United States.[12] When included in the same model, immigrant groups from highly educated home populations are still significantly less positively selected, net of distance. While this finding seems counterintuitive, it is logical if one considers the ceiling effect: among highly educated populations, immigrants' education could not possibly be much higher than average.[13] This finding also suggests that in less developed countries, the few individuals who have attained higher educations may have substantial incentives to migrate to a more developed country, such as the United States. This phenomenon, known as "brain drain," has been identified as a problem in developing countries (Glaser 1978; Grubel and Scott 1977; Vas-Zoltan 1976). Distance significantly increases the likelihood of a group being more positively selected, net of average home country educational attainment. This finding suggests one reason why Asians tend to be more highly selected than most Latin American or Caribbean groups: Asian countries are much farther away geographically than most Latin American or Caribbean countries. For example, India is almost 8000 miles away from the nearest major U.S. immigrant gateway city, while Mexico shares a border with the United States. Distance creates greater travel costs and, perhaps, psychological costs in moving to another country. Greater distance means less possibility of simply returning to the homeland. Therefore, it is very likely that Asians who migrate to the U.S. will be the most highly selective because only a few can bear the costs associated with such a drastic move.

Although it was not possible to operationalize in this analysis, United States immigration policies may also account for differences in educational selectivity by country of origin. With the 1965 Immigration Act, the two main criteria used to allow migrants to enter the United States became family reunification and occupational qualifications. Since very few Asians were allowed to enter the United States before 1965, few had family members in the United States and most could only enter under the formal credentials criteria. On the other hand, because Mexico has a long history of immigration to the United States, many Mexicans could legally migrate for family reunification purposes. Studies have shown that immigrants entering under family reunification have lower occupational statuses than those entering under employment preferences (Lobo and Salvo 1998a, 1998b). These immigrants are therefore likely to be less highly selected by education as well.

Selectivity and Changes in the Regional Origins of Immigrants

Figure 3.2 shows the selectivity of each immigrant group sorted by the region of origin and average decade of migration, to address whether immigrants from Asia and Latin America (currently the largest sending areas) are less selective than those from Europe (previously the largest sending area). The figure clearly illustrates how the regional origins of immigrants have changed over the last few decades. Most immigrant groups whose major waves arrived in the 1960's and 1970's are from Europe, while most immigrant groups who arrived more recently are from Asia, Latin America and the Caribbean. The figure

Figure 3.2. Selectivity of Migrants to the U.S., by Average Decade of Migration and Region (Net Difference Indexes)

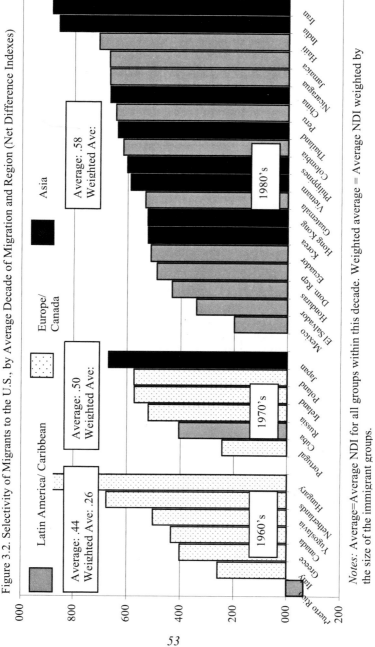

Notes: Average=Average NDI for all groups within this decade. Weighted average = Average NDI weighted by the size of the immigrant groups.

shows no clear pattern in terms of the selectivity of recent immigrant groups compared to older immigrant groups. Indeed, if anything, immigrant groups who arrived in the 1960's appear to be less positively selected than those arriving in the 1980's. The average net difference index of immigrants in the 1960's, who came mainly from Europe, was .44, compared to .58 among Asian and Latin American/Caribbean immigrants in the 1980's. Even when the average NDI is weighted by the size of the immigrant group, which accounts, for example, for the fact that over ¼ of the immigrants arriving in the 1980's were from Mexico, immigrant groups who arrived in the 1980's are not less positively selected (.44) compared to immigrant groups who arrived in the 1960's (.26). This figure suggests that immigrant groups today, especially those from Asia, are actually more likely than earlier immigrants to come from the top of the educational distribution in their country of origin. Thus, any suggestions that immigrants are currently less selective than in the past due to their changing regional origins are overstated.

Changes in the Selectivity of Mexican Immigrants Over Time

In this section, I address the question of how selectivity changes over successive waves of migrants from the same country. I examine the hypothesis that positive selectivity declines over successive waves of migrants using data on immigrants from Mexico, the largest immigrant group in the United States with the one of the longest migration histories (Bean and Stevens 2003: chap. 3; Massey 1988). It is important to note that the Mexican case is very unique compared to most other immigrant-sending countries in that it shares a border with the United States, has a long and substantial history of labor migration, and includes a large number of undocumented migrants (Bean and Stevens 2003: chap. 3).[14] While ideally I would have liked to compare the selectivity of Mexican immigrants over time to the patterns for other groups, I was unable to locate appropriate data over time for any other group.

Table 3.3 presents a series of multivariate, ordinary least-squares regression analyses to examine differences in years of schooling by migrant status among Mexicans, from 1960-2000, controlling for age and gender.[15] Focusing on the coefficients for those who migrated within the last five years,[16] we see a pattern of strong positive selection

Table 3.3. Coefficients of Determinants of Years of Schooling among Mexicans in the United States and Mexico, ages 25-64

	1960	1970	1990	2000
Recent U.S. migrant	1.178***	2.156***	1.872***	1.614***
Prior U.S. migrant (reference=nonmigrants in Mexico)	1.569***	2.504***	2.208***	2.146***
Female	-0.177***	-.392***	-.803***	-.467***
Age	-0.012***	-.025***	-.111***	-.113***
Constant	3.891***	4.897***	10.751***	11.571***
R2	0.020	0.037	0.117	0.116
N	111662	154416	307728	411006

Source: IPUMS International (Mexican and U.S. Censuses)
***p<.001

from 1960-2000. Migrants consistently averaged over one more year of schooling than Mexican nonmigrants. The migrant advantage is greatest in 1970, when they have over two more years of schooling than nonmigrants, but declines in 1990 and 2000 (although migrants in the later years still appear to have a greater advantage over nonmigrants than was true in 1960). Figure 3.2 presents two graphs describing the trends in educational selectivity among Mexican immigrants over time, using two different methods. The first panel is based on the OLS regression results in Table 3.3. Here, I plot the regression coefficients for recent migrant status standardized by the mean years of schooling of all Mexicans (migrant and nonmigrant) to facilitate the interpretation of comparisons over time. This method follows Tolnay (1998), and takes into account the rising educational attainments over the last few decades in Mexico, and thus, the fact that a one-year advantage in

1960, when Mexicans averaged 3.4 years of schooling, may be relatively larger than a one-year advantage in 2000, when the Mexican average was over seven years of schooling. The trend line indicates a sharp rise in educational selectivity among recent migrants from 1960 to 1970, perhaps due to the ending of the Bracero program in 1964, which directly recruited low-skilled laborers (Reimers: chap 4: 2005). From 1970 to 2000, however, educational selectivity appears to decline (although data is not available for 1980).

The second panel in Figure 3.3, based on comparisons of age-standardized net difference indexes from 1960-2000, presents a slightly different picture, however. We still see a sharp increase in educational selectivity from 1960 to 1970, but the pattern after 1970 is less clear. Mexican migrants decline in selectivity from 1970 to 1980, but increase from 1980 to 1990, and then decline slightly again from 1990 to 2000. Thus, instead of a pattern of declining selectivity from 1970 to 2000, as was shown when the comparison was based on mean years of schooling, a comparison based on the entire educational distribution shows little difference in the educational selectivity of recent migrants in 1970, 1990, and 2000, but lower levels of selection in 1960 and 1980. Based on these analyses, it is difficult to draw firm conclusions about the educational selectivity of Mexican immigrants over time. I find only mixed support for Massey's (1988) hypothesis that selectivity declines through each successive wave of immigrants from the same country. While the general trend is clearly *not* one of *increasing* educational selectivity over time, whether selectivity has declined since 1970 (Panel 1), or whether it has remained relatively stable (Panel 2) depends upon how education is measured. Nevertheless, it is clear that regardless of the decade of migration, Mexican immigrants are positively selected, but the level of positive selectivity (ranging from about NDI= .17 to .35) is fairly low relative to other immigrant groups (see Table 3.1).

These mixed results may have to do with the changing nature of migration from Mexico. Historically, those who leave Mexico for the U.S. have come from rural areas; now, however, a growing number are urban (Durand et al. 2001; Fussell 2004; Marcelli and Cornelius 2001; Roberts, Frank and Lozano-Ascencio 1999). Unfortunately, U.S. census data do not allow for distinctions between rural- and urban-origin Mexican immigrants. Thus, it may be possible that selectivity is declining among migrants from rural areas, where social capital

Figure 3.3. Educational Selectivity of Mexican Immigrants in the United States, 1960-2000.

A. Adjusted Differentials* between Recent Mexican Immigrants and Mexican Nonmigrants based on OLS Regressions of Years of Schooling Completed*.

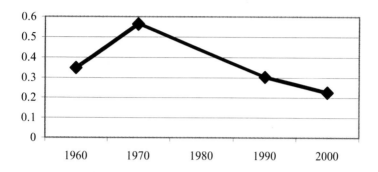

B. Age Standardized Net Difference Indexes: Comparisons of the Educational Distributions of Recent Mexican Immigrants and Mexican Nonmigrants

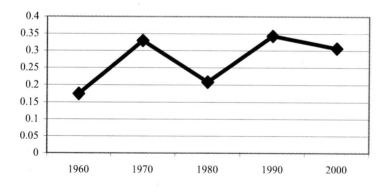

* Adjusted Differential = the ratio of the regression coefficient of recent migrant status (Table 3.3) to the mean for all Mexican-born adults ages 25-64.

mechanisms operate most strongly in reducing the costs of migration, while at the same time, urban-origin migrants who are more educated may be responding to a different set of factors (Fussell and Massey 2004). Indeed, recent research suggests that the mechanisms of cumulative causation that may lead to declining selectivity among rural Mexican migrants do not operate similarly among urban migrants (Fussell 2004; Fussell and Massey 2004). These findings suggest that future research should examine the factors influencing the changing characteristics over time of migrants from different regions in Mexico and other countries.

Conclusion

In response to Gans's (2000) appeal for more research on who immigrants are and how they differ from those who do not migrate, this chapter has been examining how immigrants' educational attainments compare to those of their nonmigrant counterparts. While scholars agree that migrants are not random samples of their home country's populations, there has been, due to a lack of empirical research, disagreement concerning how immigrants' characteristics compare to those of persons remaining in the sending society. Some scholars contend that immigrants are consistently the most educated and ambitious of their home countries, while others argue that only some immigrant groups are positively selected or that positive selectivity declines over time. This chapter takes a first step towards resolving this debate by focusing on how immigrants' educational attainments compare to those of nonmigrants.

My major findings are that, while nearly all immigrants are more highly educated than the populations remaining in their home countries, there is substantial variation in the degree of educational selectivity depending upon the country of origin and the timing of migration from a particular country. The fact that nearly all immigrant groups tend to be more educated than their nonmigrant counterparts challenges theories proposing that immigrants are only positively selected under certain conditions. Of the 32 immigrant groups studied, 31 are positively selected on education. Only Puerto Ricans are negatively selected: Puerto Rican migrants to the United States mainland tend to be less educated than Puerto Rican nonmigrants. However, this can probably be attributed to their status as United States citizens, which makes migration much less costly for Puerto Ricans than for other migrant groups.

As stated, I found that immigrants from some countries are much more highly positively selected than others. The same patterns hold for both male and female immigrants, and gender differences in selectivity within national-origin groups are generally small. Immigrants from Asia, especially those from countries with low average educational attainment levels such as India or China, tend to be more highly selected than Latin American immigrants, such as those from Mexico or the Dominican Republic. Possible factors accounting for these patterns are that Asian countries are farther away from the U.S., and that U.S. immigration policy favors the highly skilled (in the absence of family reunification).

Distance from the United States and the average educational attainment in the home country help determine immigrants' educational selectivity. Specifically, immigrants from countries that are farther from the United States (such as those in Asia) are more positively selected, which is consistent with the idea that immigrant groups facing greater barriers or costs to migration will be more highly educated relative to their home countries' populations. However, the finding that immigrants from more educated countries are less positively selected than those from countries with low levels of schooling is more counterintuitive. Part of this finding may be due to a ceiling effect created by the inclusion of some countries, such as Canada and Korea, with highly educated populations. Conversely, the finding may also be due to the inclusion of "brain drain" societies, such as India, where the general population has very little education. In such countries, it may be that those with more education have a strong incentive to migrate to more developed countries, or simply that they are the only ones with the resources to move. Future research is needed to assess these explanations. In addition, I found that some factors often thought to be predictors of selectivity, such as the level of income inequality in the origin country and whether migrants primarily left for political reasons, have no significant effect.

The changing regional origins of U.S. immigrants in the last few decades do not appear to be associated with major changes in immigrant selectivity. While previous research has suggested that recent immigrants from Asia and Latin America are less positively selected than immigrants from Europe decades ago (Borjas 1999), my findings suggest that this is not true. Contemporary immigrants are not less selected, and may even be more positively selected, than those who came from Europe in the 1960's.

Finally, I found limited support for the idea that successive waves of immigrants from Mexico are less educated relative to their home population than those who immigrated earlier. On average, Mexican immigrants arriving in the 1980's and 1990's are less positively selected than their predecessors, but their overall educational distribution is not lower. This mixed finding suggests that future research that takes into account the regional origins of immigrants within sending countries is needed to discern possible patterns of changing selectivity over time.

Understanding the selectivity of migrants is crucial to the study of immigration. While scholars agree that immigrants do not represent a random sample of their home countries' populations, it is all too easy from the vantage point of the average U.S. native to generalize immigrant characteristics to an entire national group. For example, Mexicans are generally seen as uneducated by American standards, while Indians are seen as highly educated. A look at the educational distributions of Mexico and India, however, challenges these common perceptions because *most* Indians in India have had no formal schooling compared to less than 1/3 of Mexicans in Mexico. That is, the fact that Indians who migrate to the United States are much more highly educated than those who remain in India, while Mexicans who migrate to the United States are not much more educated than those remaining in Mexico, drives the perceptions of these groups in the United States.

Having established that there is substantial variability in the educational selectivity of U.S. immigrant groups, I now turn in the remainder of the book to the implications of this fact for immigrants as they incorporate themselves into their adopted society. Specifically, I focus on educational outcomes of children of immigrants in the United States. Does the variability in selective migration help explain differences in educational outcomes among children of immigrants in the United States? The next two chapters address this question in detail, focusing on educational aspirations and expectations among youths (Chapter Four) and educational attainment among adult children of immigrants (Chapter Five).

NOTES

[1] I could not find acceptable, comparable data from Germany, England, Taiwan, Laos, Scotland, or Cambodia.

[2] While ideally, I would always use data from the year closest to the average year of migration of immigrants from that country, it was not always available. In some cases, therefore, I had to analyze data on home country populations that were several years removed from the data on U.S. immigrants from that country. However, I do not believe that this biases my results because I only compare immigrants with their home country counterparts of the same age group. Since educational attainment is fairly stable among adults (that is, by early adulthood, most individuals have attained the highest level of schooling they are ever likely to attain), selectivity among immigrants can be fairly accurately assessed even if the years of the data do not correspond, since the ages of the compared groups *do* correspond. For example, an adult who responds in 1980 that they have completed a college degree, will most likely have the same stated educational attainment in 1990, when they are 10 years older.

[3] I used this method because I did not want to over-estimate the positive selectivity of immigrants. Positive selectivity might be overestimated by using the entire distribution of immigrants for two reasons. It is well known that migration occurs in waves, and that first waves of migrants are generally thought to be the more skilled and educated than later waves (Massey 1988). Perhaps more importantly, return migration is also a common part of the migration process for many immigrants, especially those who are not successful in the United States; as many as 1/3 of immigrants to the United States eventually return to their home countries (Massey 1987b). Donato (1993) finds that those who permanently settle in the United States are more educated than those who return. Thus, limiting my analysis to only those immigrants who migrated close to the average year of migration for that particular national-origin group means that my selectivity measures are conservative; that is, I am underestimating the degree of positive selectivity from most countries.

[4] For the United States, 1% samples were downloaded directly from IPUMS International's website. A 1% sample in Mexico was available for 1970 and 1990. For 1960 and 2000 (where a 1.5% and 20% sample was available from IPUMS), I randomly sampled the appropriate number of cases, so that my final sample was 1% of the original populations.

[5] Direct standardization is a method for "controlling" for confounding factors—in this case, age. Thus, I adjust the educational attainment of nonmigrants to the age distribution of immigrants for the purpose of comparing the educational attainments of the two populations without the contaminating influence of age. The general formula is, using % college educated as an example: Age-Standardized % college educated among nonmigrants = $\sum_i M_i^n C_i^i$ where M=% college educated among nonmigrants by age and C= the proportion of immigrants in each age category. Thus, the immigrants' age distribution is used as the standard to calculate an adjusted percentage of nonmigrants who are college educated.

[6] I gratefully acknowledge an anonymous reviewer for suggesting I calculate the net difference index. Findings using a different summary measure based on comparisons of measures of central tendency and measures along specific points of the educational distribution were the same (and are available upon request). The net difference index, however, provides a simpler and more intuitive measure of educational selectivity, particularly since any immigrant group that is negatively selected would have a negative value of NDI.

[7] Specifically, if X is the percentage distribution of immigrants along educational attainment categories and Y is the percentage distribution of nonmigrants, $NDI_{xy} = pr(X>Y) - pr(Y>X)$ (Lieberson 1976: 280).

[8] I coded immigrants from Cuba, El Salvador, Guatemala, Haiti, Hungary, Iran, Nicaragua, Poland, Russia and Vietnam as political migrants (although many of these migrants may have also migrated for economic reasons).

[9] This is based on distance from the closest United States city that is considered a typical port of entry: New York, San Francisco, Los Angeles, or Miami.

[10] The gini coefficients were taken from the Deininger and Squire data set (see reference list).

[11] Although I was able to account for differences in the age compositions between home country populations and their immigrant counterparts, due to data limitations, I was not able to account for differences in the age structures between immigrant groups in calculating the selectivity measure. However, this analysis suggests that differences in the age compositions across immigrant groups do not affect my results.

[12] The variables that were not significant predictors of selectivity in the bivariate models are also not significant when included in multivariate models and do not add any explanatory power to the multivariate model (results available upon request).

[13] One way to think about this is similar to questions of socioeconomic mobility. If a child's parents are doctors, substantial upward mobility is simply not possible.

[14] Unfortunately, I am unable to distinguish between documented and undocumented immigrants with the available data. These data are based on census data that include all U.S. residents, regardless of legal status; however, undocumented immigrants are most likely underrepresented in the data. Therefore, readers should be cautious in generalizing these results to undocumented immigrants, since there may be differences in selectivity by legal status.

[15] The analyses presented in this section are based on all Mexican immigrants because the patterns did not differ for males and females (separate analyses for males and females are available from the author upon request).

[16] I focus the discussion only on recent migrants because prior migrants are likely to be a biased sample of the most successful immigrants who remain in the U.S. over a long period of time. The comparison group is Mexican nonmigrants, excluding those who ever lived abroad in 1960 and 1970, and those who were living abroad five years earlier in 1990 and 2000 (changes in the survey question do not allow for exact consistency across decades).

CHAPTER 4

Immigrant Origins and Second-Generation Ambitions

Research on status attainment has established that educational achievement has a major effect on eventual economic success, and that expectations and aspirations are key predictors of how much education a person will obtain (Duncan, Featherman, and Duncan 1972; Haller and Portes 1973; Sewell, Haller, and Portes 1969; Sewell and Hauser 1975; Sewell and Hauser 1980). Therefore, understanding how children of immigrants form educational aspirations and expectations may help to explain eventual disparities in socioeconomic attainment among national-origin groups. This chapter examines how the average educational attainment of the immigrant group relative to the home country population (educational selectivity) shapes educational aspirations and expectations among immigrants' children. By building upon the analyses of immigrants' educational selectivity in the previous chapter, this chapter brings together research on immigrant selectivity with the sociological literature on education, status attainment and second-generation adaptation. I merge these topics by examining whether and how immigrants' educational selectivity influences the educational aspirations and expectations of group members of the next generation, beyond the influence of their individual family backgrounds.

Educational Expectations, Aspirations, and Achievement among Minority Youths

The status attainment literature emphasizes the influence of family socioeconomic status on educational expectations and aspirations. Aspirations and expectations are seen as mediating the relationship between socioeconomic background and attainment, as well as exercising an independent effect on attainment (Sewell, Haller, and Portes 1969; Sewell and Hauser 1975). Within the status attainment paradigm, there are differing views of how family socioeconomic status affects aspirations, and what aspirations actually are. One view holds that aspirations are essentially achievement ambitions, and are therefore a psychological resource that individuals draw upon when considering further schooling. Family background influences aspirations through the expectations of significant people in the child's life, both those made explicitly and those indirectly alluded to by role models (Campbell 1983; Caplan, Choy, and Whitmore 1992; Davies and Kandel 1981; Sewell and Shah 1968a; Sewell and Shah 1968b). Another perspective argues that aspirations are realistic calculations of the prospects for future education (Alexander and Cook 1979; Jencks, Crouse, and Mueser 1983). According to this view, aspirations are not based on ambitions or motivations, but are based on the feasibility of further education. Family background influences aspirations because the material resources provided by the family either make further education a realistic goal or not. While the literature often uses the concepts of educational aspirations and expectations interchangeably, distinguishing between the two, as I do in this study, may clarify these two perspectives. Educational aspirations capture more general goals or ambitions for the future, while expectations more explicitly capture realistic plans for the future (Alexander and Cook 1979; Goldenberg et al 2001).

Although much of the early research showing the relationships between educational aspirations and expectations and eventual achievement was on whites only, some studies have suggested that educational aspirations and expectations are even more important predictors of educational attainment for minority youths (Kerckhoff and Campbell 1977; Portes and Wilson 1976). High educational expectations have been shown to protect Latino youths against dropping out of school (Driscoll 1999) and to predict enrollment in college for first and second-generation black, Latino, and Asian youths Glick and White 2004). However, since studies also suggest that whites and ethnic minorities encounter different mobility systems (Kerckhoff and Campbell 1977; Porter 1974; Portes and Wilson 1976), the process whereby educational aspirations and expectations are formed may differ for minorities compared to whites. Qian and Blair (1999) find that parental educational attainment and family income have stronger impacts on whites' educational aspirations than on minorities'. High aspirations among minority and low socioeconomic youths do not translate into high attainments to the same extent that they do for others (Entwisle and Hayduk 1978; Kerckhoff and Campbell 1977). Alexander, Entwisle, and Bedinger (1994) argue that educational expectations "work" best when they are based on accurate recollections of prior performance; finding that disadvantaged youths recall their prior performance less accurately and more positively than others (Alexander, Entwisle, and Bedinger 1994). Further, Asians, blacks, and Latinos all report higher educational aspirations than might be expected given their socioeconomic backgrounds (Kao and Tienda 1998).

Asians of all nationalities, in particular, have been shown to have higher educational expectations than whites, and for most Asian groups, family and individual background factors do not fully explain this finding (Goyette and Xie 1999). Goyette and Xie (1999) suggest that one possible reason for the higher educational expectations of so many diverse Asian groups may be due to selectivity on characteristics and experiences that all Asian immigrant groups share. For example, the history of Asian exclusion may have made Asian immigration very selective (Cheng and Yang 1996; Hirschman and Wong 1986). In contrast to immigrants with a longer, less restricted, history of migration to the United States, such as Mexicans, many Asian migrants could only begin to migrate under the 1965 Immigration Act's skilled worker provisions because they did not have previous family ties to draw upon for entry. Although in recent decades more Asians began to migrate under family provisions, and many Southeast Asians arrived as refugees, the historical pattern for many Asian groups has been one of skilled migration flows. To address this possibility, I examine the educational selectivity of Asian, Latino, and black immigrant groups and its impact on second-generation youths' educational expectations and aspirations.

Another possible explanation for the weaker relationship between family socioeconomic background and aspirations for minorities as compared to whites may be that minorities' aspirations are shaped more by racial than class consciousness. In other words, the collective experiences or identities of the racial/ethnic group may be more important than individual class backgrounds in shaping educational aspirations for minorities (Ogbu 1991, 2003; Qian and Blair 1999). Ogbu's (1991, 2003) notion that groups develop a collective self-identity may provide some insight, even though his framework based on a distinction between immigrant/voluntary migrants and involuntary migrants may not be entirely appropriate for analyses of the second generation: most parents of the second generation voluntarily migrated to this country. He argues that involuntary minorities, such as African Americans, develop group self-definitions that are opposed to success in mainstream educational institutions, and thus have low educational aspirations. Immigrant minorities, in contrast, develop group self-definitions that are based on a positive view of a shared heritage, thereby creating a sense of group dignity and pride (Ogbu 1974, 1991,2003). However, most empirical work shows that, contrary to Ogbu's theory, blacks have relatively high educational aspirations (Ainsworth-Darnell and Downey 1998; Hauser and Anderson 1991; Kao and Tienda 1998). Nevertheless, the idea that characteristics of immigrant groups shape the collective identity of the second generation may be significant. In particular, group selectivity may be important because if an immigrant group is composed mostly of the elite from a home country, a sense of group dignity and pride may foster the next generation's success in school. A different conception of the impact of group membership may explain the anomalous finding that, holding constant post-migration background factors, black and Latino youth have higher aspirations and expectations, yet lower achievement, than whites and Asians (Garrison 1982; Hauser and Anderson 1991; Kao 2000; Kao and Tienda 1998). Kao (2000) finds that distinct "images" of racial groups serve to maintain racial boundaries among minority youths such that minorities compare their educational performance only to others of the same race in forming their educational goals. In this chapter, I will examine the impact of group membership on educational aspirations and expectations more explicitly by investigating whether the collective characteristics of national-origin groups shape educational expectations and aspirations beyond the influence of individual background characteristics.

In addition to the importance of group characteristics and identities in shaping aspirations, studies have also shown that greater parental expectations and aspirations lead to higher educational aspirations and expectations among minority youths. One study found that the higher educational expectations of Asian parents help explain the same in Asian students as compared to whites (Goyette and Xie 1999). Similarly, Kao (2002) found that Asian parents have especially formidable aspirations in general, and that immigrant parents have even higher aspirations for their children than U.S. native parents (Kao 2002). Glick and White (2004) found that parents of immigrant students have higher educational expectations than parents of U.S. natives. Kao (2004) also finds that immigrant parents are more likely to talk with their children about college. Cheng and Starks (2002) find that Asian, black, and Latino parents' educational aspirations influence their children's educational expectations, but not as much as for their white counterparts. Like the higher than expected aspirations among minority youths, black, Hispanic, and Asian parents have been found to have higher aspirations for their children than white parents of the same socioeconomic background (Kao 2002). This chapter will examine perceptions of parental aspirations as a predictor of adolescents' educational expectations and aspirations, as well as assess the influence of immigrant group educational selectivity and socioeconomic status on parents' educational aspirations.

National Origin and Second-Generation Adaptation

The literature on second-generation adaptation suggests that it is important to look beyond family background to understand educational differences among immigrants' children. This literature emphasizes the adaptation patterns of the second generation as individuals within ethnic groups. Individual-level factors, such as family background and socioeconomic status, are not thought to be sufficient to explain adaptation patterns. For example, one of the most striking findings in Portes and Rumbaut's recent book, *Legacies*, was that "every multivariate analysis of [Children of Immigrants Longitudinal Survey] results identified nationality or ethnicity as a strong and significant predictor of virtually every adaptation outcome," even controlling for as many individual-level factors as possible (Rumbaut and Portes 2001: xvii). The authors argue that persistent national-origin differences in attainment, controlling for individual-level background factors, suggest that broader cultural or social factors affect group performance (Portes and Rumbaut 1996; Portes and Rumbaut 2001; Rumbaut and Portes 2001).

Segmented assimilation theory emphasizes the importance of group-level processes in determining the fates of contemporary immigrants and their children (Portes and Zhou 1993; Zhou 1999). While, theoretically, different outcomes might occur for different individuals within the same national-origin group, this literature has tended to emphasize the outcomes of ethnic groups as a whole: the puzzle has been to understand "how it is that different groups may come to assimilate into different segments of American society" (Portes and Rumbaut 2001: 6). To understand these diverse outcomes, scholars have emphasized the modes through which immigrant groups are incorporated into the United States. "Modes of incorporation" depend upon the contexts of reception that the group encounters upon arrival, such as U.S. policy towards the group (whether they were given refugee status and assistance, for example), prejudices of the receiving society, and characteristics of the ethnic community (Portes and MacLeod 1996; Portes and Zhou 1993: 83). Portes and Zhou's theoretical framework, which emphasizes the importance of "modes of incorporation" pertaining to entire national-origin groups, suggests that it is important to consider characteristics of the group as a whole (rather than just family and individual variables) to understand different adaptation patterns among the second generation. This chapter builds upon this idea by considering the role of immigrant group structural characteristics in explaining differences in educational aspirations and expectations among the second generation.

As suggested above, scholars have increasingly argued that it is necessary to go beyond family socioeconomic status to understand why having a certain ethnic background, such as Chinese, has a positive effect on educational achievement, while having another background, such as Mexican, has a negative effect on achievement (Hao and Bonstead-Bruns 1998; Zhou 2001). In trying to explain such ethnic differences, Zhou (2001) emphasizes how social networks based on ethnic ties within communities can provide support to certain disadvantaged groups. Zhou's (2001) work emphasizes the importance of the ethnic community in shaping the next generation's success. In particular, her work on the Vietnamese illustrates how community efforts beyond the family level can facilitate the next generation's academic success (Zhou and Bankston 1998). Bankston and Zhou (2002) point out that family ties are often disrupted by migration, while ethnic group membership is often intensified upon settling in a new country. Similarly, Portes and Rumbaut (2001) argue that the paradoxically high achievement of Southeast Asian youth can be explained by the character of these groups' ethnic communities, which are shaped by the groups' histories and modes of incorporation. Likewise, Goyette and Conchas (2002) find that relationships outside the family (i.e: non-familial social capital) play a large role in explaining variation between Vietnamese and Mexicans in educational habits.

Gibson's (1988) work on the Sikh Indians provides some evidence that relative pre-migration social status is important. In trying to uncover the reasons why second-generation Sikh Indian adolescents excel at school, even though their parents are very poor and uneducated, Gibson points to the community-wide value and encouragement of school success. But her interviews also reveal that while Sikh immigrant parents are not highly educated by U.S. standards, they were of high status in the villages from which they migrated, and this drives their high educational aspirations for the next generation. Similarly, Espiritu (2003: 365) argues that "class status is transnational." She finds that some immigrants who are very poor in the United States describe themselves as "high status" because that is their status in the home country. Immigrants' position in the social structure of their home country prior to migration, and the status attainment expectations that they bring with them, may be resources that ethnic communities can draw upon in the United States.

As I showed in the Chapter Three, nearly all immigrants are more highly educated than the populations remaining in their home countries, but immigrants vary considerably in their degree of educational selectivity depending upon the country of origin and the timing of migration from a particular country. In this chapter, I build upon these findings by addressing the question of whether these differences in the *degree* of positive educational selectivity influence educational expectations and aspirations among their children.

In sum, the literature on second-generation adaptation suggests that group-level processes are important. However, most studies do not explicitly account for group-level variables, particularly characteristics of immigrant groups prior to migration. The main contribution of this chapter is to explicitly assess the impact of immigrant group characteristics, especially educational selectivity, on second-generation individuals' educational aspirations and expectations.

DATA AND METHODS

Sample

The main data source for this study is the Children of Immigrants Longitudinal Study (CILS), a study explicitly designed to examine the adaptation processes of the second generation. CILS is a survey of U.S.-born children with at least one immigrant parent, as well as of children who immigrated at an early age, all living in San Diego, California and Miami/Ft. Lauderdale, Florida. The first survey, conducted in 1992, included 5,262 second-generation respondents who were in the 8th and 9th grades. A follow-up[1] was conducted three years later, as most were about to graduate high school; and included 4288 (81.5%) of the original respondents.[2] The results in this chapter are drawn primarily from the sample of students who participated in both waves of the study. This broad survey of the second generation was designed to assess family structure, school achievement, educational and occupational expectations and aspirations, language use and preferences, ethnic identities, and psychosocial adjustment, as well as changes in these indicators over time.

From the CILS data, I selected children of immigrants from 19 nationalities: Mexico, Cuba, Dominican Republic, Nicaragua, El Salvador, Honduras, Ecuador, Guatemala, Colombia, Peru, Korea, Hong Kong, Japan, Vietnam, Philippines, China, India, Jamaica and Haiti. I selected these 19 out of the 77 included in the CILS because they were the only nationalities with available data on immigrant group educational selectivity (as described in the previous chapter[3]). To calculate a measure of the average socioeconomic status of the immigrant group, I used data from the 1990 U.S. Census on adult immigrants from the same 19 countries whose second generation were represented in the CILS data. I merged data on the educational selectivity and socioeconomic statuses of the 19 first-generation immigrant groups to the CILS data on the corresponding second-generation children.

Measures

The two key independent variables are group-level variables describing the educational selectivity and post-migration socioeconomic status of the first-generation immigrant groups. Immigrant group educational selectivity was calculated as described in Chapter Three, using the net difference index (NDI)—a comparative measure of immigrants' and nonmigrants' educational attainments (adjusted for age) along all points of the education distribution—as the measure of selectivity. To calculate the post-migration socioeconomic status of the immigrant group, I calculated the average years of schooling, the average occupational status (Duncan SEI score), and the average income for each national-origin group using 1990 U.S. Census data (IPUMS). Since these variables were all very highly correlated, I standardized and summed these measures into a socioeconomic status scale ranging from 0 to 1. Appendix Table 4.1 lists each national-origin groups' educational selectivity (NDI) and average socioeconomic status score.

The main dependent variables in the study are students' perceptions of their parents' aspirations, and students' educational expectations and aspirations, in 1995-6, corresponding to when most of the respondents were high school seniors. I first coded a measure of the student's perception of their parents' aspirations[4] based on the question, "What is the highest level of education that your parents want you to get?" This variable was coded dichotomously depending on whether the response included a graduate degree (such as, M.A., Ph.D., M.D. or J.D.) or not. Parental aspirations are used both as a dependent variable and as an independent variable predicting youths' educational expectations and aspirations.

The survey asked two questions to assess the two distinct concepts of educational expectations and aspirations.[5] For my measure of educational expectations, I used the question, "What is the highest level of education you think you will get?" and created a dichotomous variable indicating whether the respondent expected he/she would finish college or not. To measure educational aspirations, I used the survey question, "What is the highest level of education you would like to achieve?" and created a dichotomous variable indicating whether the respondent aspired to a graduate degree or not. Since expectations tend to be more realistic goals, educational aspirations are almost always higher than expectations. Therefore, I use a higher cut-off point (graduate degree) in coding educational aspirations than educational expectations.

While I included the group measures described above based on the respondents' country of origin, I also grouped the respondents into three pan-ethnic racial groups, Latino, Asian or black. While I acknowledge that this lumps together diverse national-origin groups, such categorizations are meaningful in the U.S. context, where these terms are often used to describe these groups. Latinos include those from Mexico, Cuba, Nicaragua, Colombia, Peru, Dominican Republic, El Salvador, Guatemala, Honduras, and Ecuador. Asians include those from the Philippines, Vietnam, China, Hong Kong, Japan, Korea and India. Blacks in this sample include those from Haiti and Jamaica.

As control variables, I include the respondents' age and sex, the parents' socioeconomic status (using Portes and Rumbaut's [2001] composite indicator: the standardized unit-weighted sum of father's and mother's education, occupational status, and home ownership in 1992), whether the respondent was born in the United States, whether the respondent was fluent bilingual or not in 1992 (based on whether he/she speaks English very well and a foreign language at least well), and the respondent's grade point average in 1992.[6]

RESULTS

Descriptive Results

Table 4.1 shows the means and standard deviations of the variables used in the analysis for the three pan-ethnic racial/ethnic groups, Latinos, Asians and blacks. While the table reveals the nearly universal high educational expectations and aspirations among the three groups, there are some differences. In terms of perceptions of parents' aspirations, most Asian, black and Latino students think that their parents want them to be highly educated. According to the youths, 65% of Latino parents, 66% of Asian parents and 69% of black parents hope their child will attain a graduate degree.

Table 4.1. Means of Variables used in Analysis (standard deviations in parentheses)

	Latino	Asian	Black
Dependent Variables (Time 2, 1995-6)			
Perceptions of Parents' Aspirations: graduate degree	0.647	0.660	0.689
Expects College Degree	0.805	0.871	0.828
Aspires to Graduate Degree	0.649	0.718	0.706
Independent Variables (Time 1, 1992)			
Age	14.162	14.151	14.311
	(.848)	(.819)	(.888)
Female	0.512	0.500	0.639
Parents' Socioeconomic Status	-.089	.137	.031
	(.738)	(.653)	(.669)
Born in the United States	0.570	0.460	0.420
Fluent Bilingual	.695	0.300	0.462
Grade point average	2.372	3.049	2.455
	(.869)	(.757)	(.849)
Group-Level Independent Variables			
Immigrant Group Educational Selectivity (NDI)	0.410	0.604	0.686
	(.157)	(.038)	(.036)
Immigrant Group Socioeconomic Status	.181	0.594	0.364
(Education, Occupational Status, Income)	(.126)	(.125)	(.189)
N	2177	1115	238

Approximately 81% of second-generation Latinos expect to earn a college degree, compared to 87% of Asians and 83% of blacks. Blacks and Asians have similarly high educational aspirations: about 72% of Asians and 71% of blacks aspire to attain a graduate degree, compared to only 65% of the Latino second generation. The sample mean age for the first survey (1992) is around 14 years old. Sixty-four percent of the black respondents are female, while Asians and Latinos are more evenly divided by sex. In terms of average parental socioeconomic status, Asians (.137) rank higher than blacks (.031), and especially Latinos (-.089). The sample appears to be close to evenly divided between youths who were born in the United States and those born abroad. More than half of Latinos were born in the United States (57%) compared to 46% of Asians and 42% of blacks in the sample. There are substantial differences in terms of the levels of fluent bilingualism. Most Latinos are fluent bilingual (70%), while slightly less than half of blacks are fluent bilingual (46%), compared to only 30% of Asians. This is interesting because fluent bilingualism has been associated with such favorable educational outcomes (Feliciano 2001; Fernandez and Nielsen 1986; Stanton-Salazar and Dornbusch 1995), yet the most educationally successful group, Asians, are the least fluent bilingual. Asians have the highest grade point average in the late middle school/early high school years, with an average GPA of 3.05, compared to 2.46 among blacks and 2.37 among Latinos.

In terms of group structural characteristics, Asians and blacks are clearly more advantaged than Latinos. The average national-origin group educational selectivity (NDI) among the Latinos in the sample was only .41, compared to .60 among Asians, and .69 among blacks. The average socioeconomic status score among the immigrant groups was only .18 for the Latinos in the sample, compared to .36 for blacks, and .59 for Asians. These findings, for the first-generation national-origin groups as a whole, correspond to the average socioeconomic status among the parents of the respondents, where Asian parents had the highest socioeconomic status, followed by blacks, then Latinos. Thus, an interesting question arises regarding whether socioeconomic status at the national-origin group level will matter once I control for parental socioeconomic status. I examine these and other relationships with multivariate analyses in the next section.

Table 4.2. Odds Ratios from Logistic Regressions of Aspirations of Obtaining a Graduate Degree on Selected Independent Variables

Independent Variables	Model 1	Model 2	Model 3	Model 4	Model 5
Latino	0.724	1.08	1.851*	1.741*	1.363
Black	0.957	1.311*	1.800**	1.384+	1.364*
(ref=Asian)					
Age		.868***	.864***	0.856***	.937
Female		1.739***	1.716***	1.712***	1.380***
Parents' SES		1.790***	1.611***	1.596***	1.451***
U.S.-born		0.839	0.856	0.911	1.011
Fluent bilingual		1.467**	1.458**	1.428**	1.450**
Grade point average		1.860***	1.882***	1.884***	1.850***
Immigrant Group SES			3.818*	1.880	2.144
Immigrant Group educational selectivity (NDI)				3.139*	1.377
Perceptions of parents' aspirations					10.157***
N	3543	3543	3543	3543	3543
Pseudo R2	0.004	0.108	0.111	0.114	0.282

Robust standard errors, adjusted for clustering at national-origin group level:
+p<.10, * p<.05, ** p<.01, *** p<.001

Predictors of Educational Aspirations

In Table 4.2, I report results of logistic regression models predicting the dichotomous variable whether the respondent aspires to obtain a graduate degree or not at the second survey (when most of the respondents were high school seniors). These models contain robust standard errors that adjust for clustering at the level of the national-origin group.[7] Model 1 includes only the racial/ethnic groupings as predictors: Latinos, blacks, and Asians do not differ significantly in terms of educational aspirations. However, controlling for age, sex, parental socioeconomic status, nativity, fluent bilingualism, and 8th grade GPA in Model 2[8], blacks are actually 1.3 times more likely than Asians to aspire to obtain a graduate degree.

In Model 3, I add group socioeconomic status, one of the key independent variables. In this model, both blacks and Latinos are much more likely to aspire to a graduate degree than Asians. This suggests that the cause of lower aspirations of blacks and Latinos, in comparison to Asians, stems from the lower socioeconomic status of their immigrant groups. In fact, the strong effect of group socioeconomic status is abundantly clear: those from the highest socioeconomic status immigrant group are almost four times as likely to want a graduate education as those from the lowest.

Group educational selectivity, controlled in Model 4, also has a strong and significant effect. Respondents from the national-origin group with the highest educational selectivity are over three times as likely to aspire to a graduate degree compared to those from the least educationally select group. Controlling for group educational selectivity decreases the odds ratio for blacks (from 1.8 to 1.38) and nearly eliminates its significance. This suggests that because the blacks in this sample come from two relatively highly positively select immigrant groups (Haitians and Jamaicans), this partly accounts for their having higher aspirations than Asians, net of the control variables in Model 2. Model 4 shows that once group educational selectivity[9] is introduced to the model, the effect of group socioeconomic status is eliminated.

Finally, Model 5 adds parents' educational aspirations to the equation, which also have a strong, significant effect on child's aspirations. Those respondents who believe their parents aspire for them to obtain a graduate degree are over ten times as likely to aspire themselves to a graduate degree as those who do not think their parents have such high aspirations. Once perceptions of parents' aspirations are controlled for, group educational selectivity does not significantly affect educational aspirations, net of the control variables. This finding suggests that a significant part of the influence of immigrant group educational selectivity occurs through perceived parents' aspirations.

Predictors of Educational Expectations

Table 4.3 replicates the models in the previous analysis, with the respondent's educational expectations as the dependent variable. These models address the question of what influences the likelihood that an individual expects to attain a college degree. The first model only includes dummy variables for race, with Asian as the reference category. The odds ratios indicate that although Latinos and blacks are less likely than Asians to expect to graduate from college, as shown in the bivariate analysis; only the coefficient on blacks is significant. In Model 2, I add the control variables age, sex, parents' socioeconomic status, whether the respondent was born in the United States, whether the respondent is fluent bilingual or not, and grade point average in 1992. Adding these variables changes the odds ratios on the racial categories such that Latinos and blacks no longer significantly differ from Asians in their expectations of graduating from college. In terms of the control variables, age and being born in the United States have no effect on educational expectations. However, the other control variables all have positive effects on the likelihood of the respondent expecting to graduate college. Females are 1.4 times as likely to expect to obtain a college degree as males; as parental socioeconomic status increases, more respondents expect to graduate from college; those who are fluent bilingual are 1.7 times as likely to expect to graduate college compared to those who are not, and finally, as GPA in survey 1 increases by one point, respondents are over two times as likely to expect to graduate from college.

In Model 3, I add the average socioeconomic status of the immigrants from each respondent's national-origin group, which is one of the key independent variables. The odds ratio indicates that respondents from immigrant groups with the highest average

Table 4.3. Odds Ratios from Logistic Regressions of Expectations of Graduating from College on Selected Independent Variables

Independent Variables	Model 1	Model 2	Model 3	Model 4	Model 5	Model 6
Latino	0.626	1.104	2.211+	2.005+	1.627	1.612
Black	0.727**	1.127	1.706	1.056	0.966	1.036
(ref=Asian)						
Age		0.923	.915+	0.897*	0.960	0.959
Female		1.442**	1.409**	1.403**	1.126	1.137
Parents' SES		2.470***	2.130***	2.102***	1.951***	3.698***
U.S.-born		1.039	1.073	1.188*	1.285***	1.269**
Fluent bilingual		1.657***	1.636***	.1.578***	1.599***	1.555***
Grade point average		2.301***	2.347***	2.364***	2.282***	2.301***
Immigrant Group SES				1.507	1.438	1.644
Immigrant Group educational selectivity (NDI)			5.598*	7.573**	5.174*	2.249
Perceptions of Parents' Aspirations					4.070***	4.136***
Interaction: parents' SES and Group educational selectivity						.248**
N	3538	3538	3538	3538	3538	3538
Pseudo R2	0.007	0.157	0.163	0.167	0.225	0.228

Robust standard errors, adjusted for clustering at national-origin group level:
+p<.10, * p<.05, ** p<.01, *** p<.001

80

socioeconomic status are about 5.6 times more likely to expect their child to obtain a higher degree than those who are from the immigrant group with the lowest socioeconomic status. What is also very interesting is that when group socioeconomic status is included in the model, Latinos change from not significantly differing from Asians in their likelihood of expecting a college degree, to being over two times more likely to expect a college degree than Asians. This suggests that if Latinos were from national-origin groups with similarly high socioeconomic statuses as most Asian groups, they would have higher educational expectations than Asians or blacks. In other words, second-generation Latinos, such as Mexicans, Dominicans and Cubans, have lower educational expectations because their immigrant generations are of lower socioeconomic status than other immigrant groups. It should also be noted that the average socioeconomic status of the national-origin group significantly impacts these individuals' educational expectations, even controlling for their family background, including their own parents' socioeconomic status. Thus, group-level processes are important beyond their obvious association with family characteristics.

In Model 4, I add the other key independent variable: the educational selectivity (NDI) of the immigrant group. Once this is added to the model, the odds ratio on group socioeconomic status declines from 5.6 to 1.5, and is no longer statistically significant. This indicates that much of the influence of group socioeconomic status is due to the fact that the groups with higher socioeconomic status in the United States are also more highly selected (that is, they are more educated relative to the average educational attainment in their country of origin). Group educational selectivity[10] has a strong effect: respondents from the most highly select immigrant group are over five times more likely to expect to obtain a college degree than those from the lowest educationally select immigrant group.

Table 4.3, Model 5 includes the respondents' perceptions of whether or not their parents want them to attain a graduate degree. Parents' aspirations have a large effect on the child's educational expectations. Respondents who believe their parents want them to obtain graduate degrees are over four times more likely to expect to graduate college than those whose parents do not hope for them to obtain a graduate degree. Adding these controls to the model does not

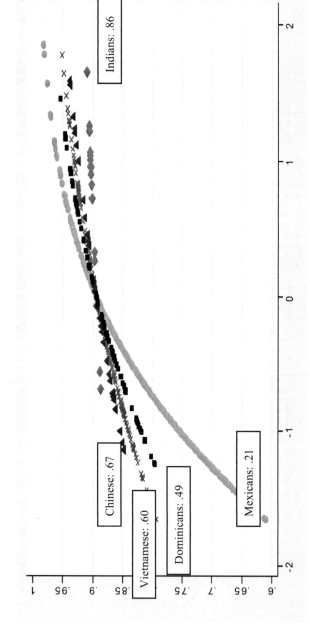

Figure 4.1. Interaction between Immigrant Group Educational Selectivity and Parents' SES

82

otherwise change the odds ratios of the variables substantially, although the odds ratio on Latinos is no longer significant. Controlling for perceptions of parents' aspirations also decreases the odds ratio on group educational selectivity. This suggests that group educational selectivity influences the aspirations that parents have of their children, and it is partly through this mechanism that this group-level characteristic affects expectations among the second generation. I will explore this idea further in the next section.

Model 6 introduces an interaction effect between parents' socioeconomic status and group educational selectivity. The interaction effect is significant, indicating that the effect of parents' socioeconomic status on children's educational expectations depends upon the level of group educational selectivity. Figure 4.1 illustrates this interaction effect by using five groups who have varying average levels of educational selectivity, as examples. The figure is based on Table 4.3, Model 6, with all independent variables (except parents' socioeconomic status and group educational selectivity) set to their means. The figure shows that for the least educationally select group, Mexicans (NDI=.21), the predicted probability of expecting to attain a college degree varies greatly depending on the parents' socioeconomic status (indicated by the steepness of the curve). That is, Mexican youths from families with very low socioeconomic status have relatively low educational expectations (around 60% expect a college degree), while Mexican youths from high socioeconomic status families have very high educational expectations (close to 100%). In contrast, for the most highly selected immigrant group, Indians (NDI=.86), the predicted probability of expecting a college degree does not seem to depend at all on their parents' socioeconomic status. Of course, there is a relationship between group educational selectivity and parental socioeconomic status, such that there are no Indian respondents whose parents are of extremely low socioeconomic status. However, Vietnamese respondents' parents range from having very low to very high socioeconomic statuses as well. Nevertheless, because their immigrant group's educational selectivity is fairly high, college expectations among Vietnamese youths do not vary much based on parental socioeconomic status. Thus, while these Vietnamese youths from lower socioeconomic backgrounds have slightly lower college expectations than those from higher socioeconomic backgrounds, the relationship is not nearly as strong as it is for Mexican youths: the predicted probabilities of expecting a college degree only range from around 81% to 95% among Vietnamese youths. These findings suggest that even if their parents are of low socioeconomic status, youths from immigrant groups that are relatively highly educationally selected will have high educational expectations.

Predictors of Perceptions of Parents' Aspirations

Table 4.4 shows five models predicting parents' educational aspirations for their children (as perceived by the child). The dependent variable is whether or not their parents aspire for the respondents to attain a graduate degree. Model 1 shows that parents of Latino, black, and Asian second-generation adolescents do not significantly differ in this case. Model 2 adds several control variables, showing that parental aspirations are lower for older students, and higher for females, those with higher socioeconomic status parents, those who are fluent bilingual, and those who have a higher grade point average (during survey 1). Once these controls are added, black students actually perceive their parents to have higher educational aspirations for them than do Asian students.

Model 3 adds the average socioeconomic status of the immigrant group. Controlling for group socioeconomic status, Latino parents are actually now nearly two times as likely to aspire for their children to attain a graduate degree as Asian parents, at least as perceived by the child. Group socioeconomic status has a strong and significant effect: parents from immigrant groups of the highest socioeconomic status (even if they are not of high socioeconomic status themselves) are over three times as likely to aspire for their children to attain a graduate degree as those parents from the lowest socioeconomic status immigrant group.

Model 4 adds the average educational selectivity of the immigrant group to the model. Parents from the most highly positively select immigrant group are over six times as likely to aspire for their children to obtain a college degree compared to parents from the least select immigrant group. Consistent with the findings for educational aspirations and expectations, once group educational selectivity is controlled for, the effect of group socioeconomic status disappears, suggesting that group socioeconomic status only matters because of its

Table 4.4. Odds Ratios from Logistic Regressions of Perceptions of Parents' Aspirations of Respondent Obtaining a Graduate Degree

Independent Variables	Model 1	Model 2	Model 3	Model 4	Model 5
Latino	0.944	1.261	1.985*	1.820***	1.595***
Black	1.163	1.372**	1.791*	1.189	1.067
(ref=Asian)					
Age		.829***	.826***	.814***	.824***
Female		1.735***	1.715***	1.712***	1.542**
Parents' SES		1.610***	1.474***	1.452***	1.301**
U.S.-born		.724+	.734*	0.809	0.827
Fluent bilingual		1.205*	1.199+	1.158	1.080
Grade point average		1.378***	1.340***	1.391***	1.265**
Immigrant Group SES				1.020	.861
Immigrant Group educational selectivity (NDI)			3.088*	6.282***	5.691***
Child's aspirations					2.507***
N	3546	3546	3546	3546	3546
Pseudo R2	0.001	0.059	0.062	0.066	0.094

Robust standard errors, adjusted for clustering at national-origin group level:
+p<.10, * p<.05, ** p<.01, *** p<.001

85

correlation with selectivity. Also, Latino parents are still 1.8 times as likely to aspire for their children to graduate from college as Asian parents, while the odds ratio for blacks declines substantially. This suggests that blacks' perceptions of their parents' high aspirations are due to the high educational selectivity of their immigrant generation. Finally, controlling for the child's own educational aspirations (in Model 5) does not change the previous results: group educational selectivity remains a strong and significant predictor of perceived parental aspirations.

Summary and Discussion

This chapter points to the importance of distinguishing between educational aspirations, as general future goals, and expectations, as more realistic future plans. The ambiguity in the status attainment literature as to whether family socioeconomic status matters because it shapes achievement ambitions through family members' expectations, or simply because family socioeconomic status captures material resources, can be clarified by examining both aspirations and expectations. My findings suggest that both perspectives are valid, depending upon the outcome of interest. With *aspirations* as the outcome, a social-psychological view of the role of family background is supported. That is, much of the influence of family socioeconomic status, as well as immigrant group educational selectivity, is mediated by perceptions of parents' aspirations. The statistical significance of family socioeconomic status declines substantially once perceptions of parents' aspirations are included in the model, suggesting that higher socioeconomic status is beneficial because students perceive their parents to have greater aspirations for them. In other words, what students think their parents hope for them is extremely important, and is partly influenced by family socioeconomic status. Further, the significance of group educational selectivity is eliminated once perceptions of parents' aspirations are included, suggesting that higher group educational selectivity is also beneficial because it facilitates higher perceived parental aspirations. Thus, parental aspirations are more important than group selectivity in determining adolescents' aspirations, but group selectivity is an important determinant of parents' aspirations. In contrast, when educational *expectations* are the outcome, socioeconomic status is strongly significant, even controlling for parents' aspirations; perceived parental aspirations also do not eliminate the role of group educational selectivity in forming educational expectations. These findings suggest that family background and group characteristics influence *expectations* for the future, not only because they help form ambitions, but because they capture real material resources that make further education a feasible goal or not.

Distinguishing between educational aspirations and expectations is also important because the effects of racial/ethnic group membership vary depending upon the outcome. While the data do not allow for comparisons with whites, the findings show that, contrary to the suggestions of prior research, Asians do not have higher aspirations than Latinos or blacks (at least among the second generation). Asians, however, do have higher educational *expectations* than blacks and Latinos, but this is explained by the more favorable parental socioeconomic statuses and other individual characteristics of Asians. Blacks, controlling for individual characteristics, have higher educational aspirations, but not expectations, than Asians. One likely explanation for this pattern is that, because expectations are more realistic goals, blacks' experiences of discrimination negatively affect their expectations, even while they maintain their high educational aspirations. The results also suggest that the Latino second generation and their parents would have much higher educational expectations and aspirations if it weren't for the lower selectivity and socioeconomic status of their immigrant groups. In fact, controlling for immigrant group characteristics, second-generation Latino youths actually had higher perceived parental aspirations than either Asians or blacks.

The national-origin group-level structural characteristics examined here—educational selectivity and socioeconomic status—appear to play a part in influencing educational aspirations and expectations among the second generation. Some of this influence works through the influence of parents, or at least the students' perceptions of their parents' desires for them. That is, parents' aspirations are not just based on what their relative class standing was prior to migration, or what their own socioeconomic status is, but on the prior relative class standing of the entire immigrant generation who have migrated to the United States from their country. Those from immigrant groups who are more highly selected have higher aspirations for their children's educational attainment. Parents' aspirations, in turn, shape the educational expectations, and especially, aspirations of their children, such that children with parents who have higher hopes for their educational attainment develop higher educational aspirations and expectations themselves. The findings also show that national-origin group educational selectivity directly affects educational expectations for second-generation youths, beyond just its effects on parents' aspirations.

That characteristics of groups influence individual outcomes for Asian, black, and Latino second-generation adolescents suggests one reason why the status attainment process may differ for minorities and whites. At least for children of immigrants, individual family socioeconomic status may matter less in shaping their educational aspirations and expectations than for whites because second-generation adolescents are influenced by characteristics of the immigrant generation beyond the influence of their parents.

Although understanding precisely how and why national-origin group educational selectivity shapes individuals' aspirations and expectations is a complex topic worth further research, two explanations suggested by the literature provide a starting point. One possibility draws upon Ogbu's notion that groups develop collective identities (Ogbu 1991; Ogbu 2003). National-origin educational selectivity may help create a collective identity among group members, and those group reputations or group self-definitions may help shape educational outcomes among the second generation. For example, highly educationally select immigrant groups' identities may be based on a sense that they are entitled to mainstream success, given their place in their home countries' class system prior to migration.

The second explanation is drawn from segmented assimilation theory, which emphasizes the role of the ethnic community in shaping second-generation adaptation (Portes and Zhou 1993; Zhou and Bankston 1998). The findings here suggest that collective experiences are important in shaping not only immigrants' experiences, but those of their children as well. Thus, youths may also be influenced by their ethnic community members, other than their parents, in forming expectations of the future. Immigrant groups that were of higher status in their home country (and thus more educationally select) may have higher expectations for their next generation, and may foster the next generation's educational motivation through community activities and values. My finding that the influence of parents' socioeconomic status on educational expectations depends upon the educational selectivity of the immigrant group supports this interpretation. This suggests that even if parents have limited material resources, those from highly selected immigrant groups will still have higher educational expectations, perhaps because of the added resources provided by a highly select ethnic community.

In sum, the findings of this study support the segmented assimilation theory's view that group-level characteristics are important in shaping the adaptation process for second-generation youths, and that these characteristics matter above and beyond the influence of individual family backgrounds. Further, the findings in this chapter highlight the interaction effects between group and individual-level factors, which the segmented assimilation literature discusses, but rarely operationalizes. At least for expectations of graduating from college, the effect of parents' socioeconomic status depends upon the selectivity of the immigrant group to which they belong. This suggests one possible reason why children of certain immigrants, such as the Vietnamese, are often quite successful in school even if they come from poor families. Vietnamese youths' educational expectations are strongly influenced by the relatively high educational selectivity of their immigrant group, such that their own family background is not as determinative as it is for other groups who are less selective (such as Mexicans). Structural characteristics of the immigrant group—especially their relative pre-migration education—influence the educational aspirations and expectations of second-generation youths, and do so partly by shaping the educational aspirations of immigrant parents. These findings suggest that group-level characteristics matter above and beyond their association with individual family background characteristics and that greater attention needs to be drawn to the effects of ethnic communities and group identities in understanding the adaptation processes of the second generation.

In spite of their strength, the findings here are limited in that I was only able to examine outcomes among adolescents who are still of high-school age with the CILS data. It remains unclear whether high educational aspirations and expectations will translate into high educational attainments, and whether the effects of selectivity apply to actual educational attainments. To address these questions, I turn in the next chapter to analyses of educational attainment among adult children of immigrants.

NOTES

[1] A third follow-up was conducted in 2000-2001, as the respondents were entering into adulthood. Unfortunately, as of this writing, these data are not yet publicly available.

[2] Portes and Rumbaut (2001) present several analyses to show that there is no serious bias in the follow-up sample. For the most part, the follow-up survey respondents appear similar to the original survey respondents on indicators such as nativity, citizenship, parents' socioeconomic status, sex etc. However, there is a slight tendency for children from families with both parents present to be overrepresented in the follow-up survey.

[3] Only 19 out of the 32 groups for which I had gathered data (described in Chapter 3) were present in sizeable numbers in the CILS data.

[4] The CILS includes a parental survey for a portion of the respondents. However, parents of only a portion of the respondents who answered the second follow-up survey were surveyed. Therefore, it would decrease the sample sizes substantially if I included parents' responses. Further, parents were not asked about their aspirations for their child's education, only their expectations. Therefore, I could not compare how well the students' perceptions of their parents' aspirations compared with their parents' actual aspirations. I did compare the students' perceptions of their parents' aspirations with the parents' expectations, for those with available data. The two are positively correlated (.22), but students' perceptions of their parents' desires for them are generally much higher than the parents' expectations. For example, 66% of the students (with parental survey data) thought that their parents wanted them to obtain a graduate degree, but only 36% of parents expected their child to obtain a graduate degree. I suspect that a child's own educational expectations and aspirations are likely to be shaped more by their perceptions of what they *think* their parents want for them, regardless of what their parents' aspirations actually are (although they related). Therefore, it is appropriate to use the students' perceptions of their parents' aspirations as a predictor and as a dependent variable. However, readers should be cautioned that students' perceptions may not match parents' actual aspirations. Indeed, Davies and Kandel (1981) show that actual parents' aspirations exert an effect on their child's aspirations, apart from the child's own perceptions. These authors also argue that perceptions are partly influenced by the perceiver's own aspirations, thus introducing potential endogeneity problems of which readers should be aware.

[5] The two concepts are related, of course, such that students who have high educational expectations nearly always have high aspirations. The correlation between the original variables is .68. However, the concepts are distinct in that respondents often aspire to higher educational attainments than they believe are realistic, and for this reason, I analyze them separately. For example, 35% of those who aspire to a graduate degree do not expect to actually attain a graduate degree.

[6] GPA was obtained from student records.

[7] I follow a similar method as that employed by Borjas (2001) of using a "mixed" regression model with the dependent variable defined at the individual-level, while some of the independent variables are defined at the group level. Since the residuals among the observations within the same national-origin group are correlated, I correct the standard errors to account for the structure of the data using STATA's cluster option in logistic regression models.

[8] I also tried additional variables—years in the U.S., two-parent home, and limited bilingual—that consistently had no effect on the models and thus are not included here.

[9] I ran a model with an interaction between group educational selectivity and parental socioeconomic status, but the interaction was not significant.

[10] In separate analyses, available upon request, I also calculated the educational selectivity of the respondent's parents themselves (i.e.: the difference between their parents' educational attainment and that of the average in their home country). This variable (I tried several different codings) does not significantly impact children's expectations, once parents' socioeconomic status is included in the model. Further, its inclusion does not affect the odds ratio on group educational selectivity, which still significantly influenced educational expectations.

CHAPTER 5

Immigrant Origins and Second-Generation Attainment

This chapter continues the argument that the selective nature of immigrants' migration, in terms of how their educational attainments compare to nonmigrants in their home countries, helps explain educational attainment differences among immigrants' children. The previous chapter explored the influences of immigrants' educational selectivity on the aspirations and expectations of adolescents of the next generation. It found that selectivity shapes children's aspirations by influencing perceptions of their parents' aspirations for them, and also has a direct positive relationship with educational expectations. As I maintain in that chapter, educational expectations have been established as an important predictor of subsequent educational attainment (Duncan, Featherman, and Duncan 1972; Haller and Portes 1973; Sewell, Haller, and Portes 1969; Sewell and Hauser 1975; Sewell and Hauser 1980). Nevertheless, educational expectations are frequently not realized (Hanson 1994). Thus, educational expectations are at best a rough indicator of eventual schooling outcomes. For example, the high educational expectations and aspirations of Mexican adolescents do not seem to conform to their patterns of educational attainment as adults (St. Hilaire 2002). Since educational expectations are not a perfect predictor of attainment, and educational attainment is the most important predictor of success in U.S. labor markets (Duncan, Featherman, and Duncan 1972), I focus this chapter on years of schooling completed, high school graduation, and college attendance, all of which are clear educational outcomes among adult children of immigrants.

Class Reproduction from Immigrants to the Next Generation

In proposing a link between immigrants' educational selection—where immigrants ranked within their home country's educational stratification system—and educational outcomes among immigrants' children, I suggest that ethnic differences in educational success among immigrants' children can partly be attributed to the reproduction of pre-migration class structures in the United States. Thus, I am addressing the question of whether education creates social mobility and opportunities or whether education merely serves to reproduce the existing social class structure. Scholars such as Bourdieu (1973), Bowles and Gintis (1976), and Willis (1977) argue that, rather than allowing for upward mobility, education actually perpetuates existing inequalities. Rather than equalizing opportunities for those who come from disadvantaged backgrounds, these scholars argue that the educational system, through formal means such as tracking, and informal means such as rewarding certain cultural practices, places students on a pathway to replicate the class status of their family. According to this view, immigrants who come to the United States seeking better educational opportunities for their children may be disappointed by the realities of limited social mobility.

While immigrants' children almost always attain more schooling in absolute terms than their parents (Farley and Alba 2002), in relative terms they may just be reproducing their parents' pre-migration class status. In a broad view, the absolute level of education, such as having graduated high school, should be compared to the context in which the specific degree is attained. Neglecting educational selectivity, or relative educational attainment, assumes that completing high school in one country, for example, where only 10% of the population does so means the same as in another country where 80% of the population does so. Because educational opportunities differ substantially by country, immigrants who do not have high educational credentials by American standards may, in fact, be quite selective relative to the general populations in their home countries (Lieberson 1980: 213-214). Stratification models may therefore need to be revised for immigrants' children to reflect the different meanings of educational attainment for different immigrant groups.

As suggested by the previous chapter, educational selectivity may affect children's educational outcomes through family background and social, cultural and ethnic capital. In this way, parents' education is the single most important determinant of children's schooling for reasons that go beyond its economic relationship to occupational status and income (Blau and Duncan 1967; Hirschman and Falcon 1985; Jencks et al. 1972). For instance, children of highly educated parents may perceive more pressure to continue in school even if they are not academically oriented (Jencks et al. 1972: 138; Sewell, Haller, and Ohlendorf 1970). Such non-economic benefits of belonging to a highly selective immigrant group are reinforced by the previous chapter, which finds that immigrant selectivity has a strong effect on youths' perceptions of their parents' aspirations for them: adolescents from highly selective immigrant groups feel that their parents' aspirations for them are extremely high. Furthermore, children from middle class or upper class families may have more cultural capital, which includes resources and advantages such as attitudes, speaking styles, and interaction skills that are rewarded in school (Bourdieu 1973; Bourdieu and Passeron 1977). As suggested, these non-economic forms of capital might transfer across borders, even if immigrant parents are not that educated by U.S. standards. For example, immigrants who were of high status in the home country may facilitate the achievement of the next generation in order to attain a similar class position in the United States.

The segmented assimilation literature suggests that ethnic capital—social or cultural capital provided by the ethnic community, and characteristic of an entire immigrant group—may influence the next generation's educational success (Borjas 1992a; Portes and Rumbaut 2001, 1996; Zhou and Bankston 1998, 1994). Similarly, Borjas (1992a: 126) writes, "persons who grow up in high-quality ethnic environments will, on average, be exposed to social, cultural, and economic factors that increase their productivity when they grow up." Wilson's (1990) work on the underclass also notes the importance of these resources. He argues that the prospects of young black males in inner city neighborhoods are poor because they are not exposed to "mainstream role models that keep alive the perception that education is meaningful [and] that steady employment is a viable alternative to welfare" (Wilson 1990: 56). Furthermore, Borjas (1992a) shows that the skills of the second generation depend not only on the parents' skills, but equally as much on the average skills of the entire immigrant generation. He finds that ethnic capital, which he measures as the average earnings of the immigrant group, is an important predictor of the earnings of the second generation and slows down the convergence of ethnic socioeconomic differences across generations (Borjas 1993, 1992a).

I argue that the average educational selectivity of the immigrant generation can be thought of as a form of ethnic capital that influences educational attainment among the second generation. This chapter thus brings together ideas from the literatures on immigrant selectivity, class reproduction, and second-generation adaptation to try to understand what accounts for ethnic and racial differences in educational attainment among the new second generation.

Analysis Strategy

This chapter addresses two related questions. First, it looks at whether immigrants' educational selectivity helps explain why some ethnic groups obtain higher amounts of schooling, on average, than others. In this case, a group-level analysis is an appropriate test of the selectivity hypothesis. Following Borjas (1993), I conduct ordinary least squares regression analyses on aggregate national-origin groups to ascertain whether selectivity affects the average educational attainment of the one and a half generation—those who migrated as children before the age of 11—and second-generation groups, net of the immigrant group's average socioeconomic status. I employ a similar method to Borjas (1993), using intercensal comparisons to increase the likelihood that the groups of immigrants are the parents of the second generation.[1]

The second issue I address is whether or not immigrants' educational selectivity helps explain why individual children of immigrants from certain ethnic/racial groups are more or less likely to attain educational success (as measured by high school graduation and college attendance). To this end, I examine differences across four broad pan-ethnic/racial groups: whites (European/Canadian origin), blacks (West Indian origins), Asians (Asian origin), and Latinos (Latin American or Spanish-speaking Caribbean origins). Clearly, these are umbrellas for very diverse national-origin groups. However, because these groups tend to get lumped together when they come to the United States, the categories are meaningful. For example, the terms "Asian excellence" and "Latino underachievement" are often used in both academic and popular circles. At the individual level, I conduct logistic regression analyses on 1.5 and second-generation adults to ascertain whether including the immigrant group's educational selectivity as an independent variable explains the significance of membership in a white, black, Asian, or Latino group.

To supplement the primary findings of the study, and to provide further evidence of whether selective migration matters for children of immigrants' educational adaptation, I include a descriptive examination of whether changes in selectivity among Mexican immigrants over time correspond to similar changes in educational attainment among their children. The reader should be cautioned that these are modest tests of the selectivity hypothesis. Given the limitations of the data, I can only examine whether there is an empirical relationship between the pre-migration educational position of immigrant groups and the attainment of immigrants' children: I cannot explore in detail the mechanisms through which group selectivity might influence the education of second-generation individuals. However, the previous chapter suggests that one possible mechanism for this influence is through the conditioning of educational aspirations and expectations of both parents and children.

DATA AND VARIABLES

To examine educational attainment outcomes among adult children of immigrants, including years of schooling completed, high school graduation, and college attendance, I created extracts from the IPUMS and the Current Population Survey (CPS) on children of immigrants ages 20-40[2] from 32 countries. I calculated this variable for both the 1.5 generation, who migrated as children before the age of 11, and the second generation, who were born of at least one immigrant parent in the United States. The ethnic group of the second generation is defined by the father's place of birth, or, if only the mother was born abroad, the mother's place of birth. For the 1.5 generation, I used 1990 IPUMS data, as it is the only dataset with sufficient sample sizes. For the second generation, I used the 1997-2001 March Current Population Surveys: the CPS, unlike the Census, has a question about parents' nativity which allows me to directly identify U.S.-born children of immigrants (see Farley and Alba (2002) for a discussion of the utility of the CPS to examine the second generation). I combined the non-repeated cases across these 5 years in the CPS to create a dataset of the second generation as of the late 1990's/early 2000's. Table 5.1 shows the dependent variables for the 1.5 and second generation of each national-origin group. The independent variables in this chapter build upon the measure of educational selectivity that I calculated for the 32 immigrant groups in Chapter Three. As described in more detail in that chapter, I calculated a net difference index (NDI) that compares the overall distributions of educational attainment of immigrants vs. their nonmigrant home country counterparts. In addition, as a key control variable, I use the average socioeconomic status of the immigrant group, as calculated in Chapter Four. This measure was calculated using the average years of schooling, average occupational status (Duncan SEI score), and the average income for each national-origin group by standardizing and summing these highly correlated measures into a socioeconomic status scale ranging from 0 to 1. Table 5.1 lists these independent variables for each national-origin group.

RESULTS: GROUP-LEVEL

Descriptive Results

As previously mentioned, Table 5.1 shows the main independent and dependent variables used in the group-level analysis, sorted by the country of origin. It illustrates the substantial variability in selectivity, socioeconomic status, and educational attainment among the 32 groups in the study. One and a half generation and second-generation Indians have the highest levels of educational attainment, whether measured by mean years of schooling, percent high school graduates, or percent that have attended some college. At the other end of the spectrum, Mexicans have among the lowest levels of attainment. For example, 1.5-generation Indians average 14.6 years of schooling, 98% are high school graduates, and 88% have attended at least some college. In contrast, 1.5-generation Mexicans average 11.2 years of schooling, only 59% are high school graduates, and only 32% have at least some college education. For these groups and most others, educational

Table 5.1. Means of Independent and Dependent Variables by National Origin
*NDI = Net Difference Index (Educational Selectivity)

COUNTRY	IND. VAR		DEPENDENT VARIABLES							
			1990 Census, 1.5 generation, ages 20-40				1997-2001 CPS, 2nd generation, ages 20-40			
	NDI*	SES	Ave. Yrs	% HS grad	% Some college	N	Ave. Yrs	% HS grad	% Some college	N
Canada	.434	0.749	13.7	93.1	67.5	1227	13.8	93.5	71.1	497
China	.671	0.380	13.5	85.7	70.3	91	15.4	97.9	90.1	146
Colombia	.625	0.397	13.5	87.6	68.4	193	13.5	95.0	70.9	105
Cuba	.399	0.227	13.4	87.9	62.8	1088	14.2	95.2	70.8	332
Dom.Republ.	.490	0.176	12.6	77.3	54.6	194	13.1	87.0	58.2	190
Ecuador	.496	0.287	13.0	82.3	60.0	130	13.5	90.0	70.9	62
El Salvador	.350	0.057	11.9	71.7	50.0	106	13.0	87.1	54.1	183
Greece	.409	0.271	13.2	82.7	57.9	197	14.0	97.8	74.8	108
Guatemala	.551	0.062	12.5	74.7	57.1	91	13.1	86.8	61.8	43
Haiti	.720	0.187	13.5	88.5	72.9	96	14.0	100.0	81.7	42
Honduras	.454	0.093	12.7	90.4	65.4	52	13.4	95.4	69.8	31
Hong Kong	.612	0.772	14.4	97.7	85.1	215	13.7	87.9	74.4	23
Hungary	.885	0.646	14.6	98.0	71.4	49	14.0	97.4	68.6	60
India	.859	1.000	14.6	98.0	88.4	198	15.4	100.0	90.3	91
Iran	.884	0.764	14.0	97.0	76.1	67	14.5	90.7	78.8	33
Ireland	.572	0.699	13.9	94.0	65.7	67	14.4	97.0	79.2	158
Italy	.258	0.453	13.0	85.6	53.2	626	14.0	97.5	69.5	459
Jamaica	.678	0.567	13.4	87.1	62.2	217	13.9	92.5	81.4	62
Japan	.670	0.766	13.7	94.0	71.7	814	14.3	95.8	74.5	101
Korea	.525	0.575	13.9	96.3	79.3	300	14.5	100.0	90.1	60
Mexico	.208	0.000	11.2	59.3	31.9	3502	12.4	78.5	44.0	2582
Netherlands	.685	0.861	13.9	94.6	73.2	149	14.4	100.0	88.7	82
Nicaragua	.670	0.285	12.6	83.3	51.9	54	13.3	91.9	74.9	46
Peru	.645	0.427	13.1	90.1	69.1	81	13.9	95.4	81.0	57
Philippines	.597	0.658	13.5	93.3	74.4	653	13.5	96.9	74.2	249
Poland	.573	0.540	12.8	84.0	51.2	131	14.4	95.7	72.1	113
Portugal	.231	0.190	12.2	76.7	38.4	245	13.0	86.9	58.8	93
Puerto Rico	-.064	0.088	11.7	63.9	33.8	1457	12.4	76.9	44.1	1175
Thailand	.648	0.463	13.0	86.9	59.0	61	13.2	67.8	58.2	30
Russia	.365	0.776	13.4	94.6	71.4	56	14.3	100.0	82.1	26
Vietnam	.595	0.423	12.9	86.0	68.6	242	14.1	100.0	90.3	24
Yugoslavia	.502	0.479	13.0	86.5	57.3	96	13.4	87.3	68.0	47

attainment rates are slightly higher among the second generation than the 1.5 generation, most likely because the data for the second generation come from a later time period.

The relationship between the immigrant groups' educational selectivity (NDI) and socioeconomic score is particularly important because selective migration may not capture anything above and beyond an immigrant groups' socioeconomic status in the United States. In Table 5.2, I show a cross-tabulation of dichotomous measures of immigrant group selectivity and socioeconomic status, based on whether the immigrant group was above or below the median. The table shows that while most groups correspond on both indicators (are both low or both high in selectivity and socioeconomic status), a substantial minority of groups diverges on the two measures. For example, Mexicans and Puerto Ricans both have very low educational selectivity and socioeconomic status. In fact, Puerto Rican migrants are the only group that is negatively selected (-.064, Table 5.1) and they have the second-lowest socioeconomic status (0.88, Table 5.1). Mexicans have the third lowest NDI (.208, Table 5.1) and the lowest socioeconomic status score (0.00, Table 5.1). Conversely, Indians have very high selectivity (.859, Table 5.1), and also very high socioeconomic status (1.00, Table 5.1). In contrast, other groups, such as Canadians and Russians, have high socioeconomic status, but low selectivity. These immigrant groups come from countries with high overall educational attainment levels, which, due to a ceiling effect, necessarily means the immigrants will not be that highly selected. Further, some groups; including immigrants from Nicaragua, Haiti and China, are highly selected, but are of low overall socioeconomic status. These immigrants are much more highly educated relative to their home countries' populations, but do not have high educational attainment, occupational statuses or incomes by American standards.

Table 5.2 also shows the college attendance outcome for the 1.5 and second-generation groups in each cell. Not surprisingly, those from immigrant groups with both low selectivity and low socioeconomic status have the lowest college attendance rates (51.18% for the 1.5 generation and 60.73% for the second generation). Among the 1.5 generation, those from immigrant groups with both high socioeconomic status and high selectivity have the highest college attendance rates (71.28%). However, college attendance rates for those from immigrant groups with high selectivity, but low socioeconomic status are similar

Table 5.2. Average Socioeconomic Status by Educational Selectivity and Percent of Next Generation with Some College Attainment, 32 Origin Countries

	Low Average Socioeconomic Status	**High Average Socioeconomic Status**
Low Average Selectivity	Cuba, Dominican Republic, Ecuador, El Salvador, Greece, Guatemala, Honduras, Mexico, Portugal, Puerto Rico	Canada, Ireland, Italy, Korea, Russia, Yugoslavia
	Average College Attendance Rate of these origin countries:	*Average College Attendance Rate of: these origin countries*
	1.5 gen: **51.2** % 2nd gen: **60.7** %	1.5 gen: **65.7** % 2nd gen: **76.7** %
High Average Selectivity	China, Colombia, Haiti, Nicaragua, Peru, Vietnam	Hong Kong, Hungary, India, Iran, Jamaica, Japan, Netherlands, Philippines, Poland, Thailand
	Average College Attendance Rate of these origin countries:	*Average College Attendance Rate of these origin countries:*
	1.5 gen: **66.9** % 2nd gen: **81.5** %	1.5 gen: **71.3** % 2nd gen: **76.1** %

to those of high socioeconomic status, but low selectivity. Interestingly, among the second generation, those immigrant groups with high selectivity and low socioeconomic status have higher college attendance rates (81.5%), exceeding even those with both high selectivity and high socioeconomic status (76.1%). This descriptive analysis shows that children of immigrant groups with high selectivity are doing quite well, even if those groups are of low socioeconomic status in the United States (this includes people from China, Colombia, Haiti, Nicaragua, Peru and Vietnam). Keep in mind, however, that the dichotomous measures of selectivity and socioeconomic status are quite simplified. For example, this table suggests a great deal of overlap between the two: both measures are in fact highly correlated (.60). Nevertheless, only two groups, Mexicans and Puerto Ricans, are in both the lowest quartile of socioeconomic status and selectivity, and only one group, Indians, is in the highest quartile of both indicators. Thus, I turn now to regression analyses that preserve the full range of both indicators.

Regression Results: The 1.5 Generation

Table 5.3 shows regression results for the determinants of three educational outcomes among 1.5-generation immigrant groups: mean years of schooling, percent college educated, and percent high school graduates. I begin with a model that includes the average socioeconomic status of the immigrant group as the only predictor of each educational outcome. Then, in Model 2, I include immigrants' educational selectivity to see if it adds any significant explanatory power.[3] Table 5.3, Model 1, shows that the immigrant group's average socioeconomic status is a strong predictor of all three educational attainment outcomes for 1.5-generation groups. Thus, the national-origin group with the highest immigrant socioeconomic status score (coded 1), has 2.37 more years of schooling than the group with the lowest socioeconomic status score (coded 0), and this variable explains 67% of the variance in average years of schooling among 1.5-generation groups. Less variance in the percent college educated (53%) is explained by immigrant socioeconomic status, while socioeconomic status also explains 67% of the variance in the percentage of high school graduates. The coefficients reveal that the national-origin group with the highest average immigrant socioeconomic status has nearly

Table 5.3. Coefficients of Models of the Determinants of Educational Attainment among 1.5-Generation Immigrant Groups in the United States, 1990 (N=32) (standard errors in parentheses)

Independent Variables	Mean Years of Schooling		% Some College		% H.S. Graduates	
	Model 1	Model 2	Model 1	Model 2	Model 1	Model 2
Immigrant Generation's Socioeconomic Status (Occupational Status, Income, Education)	2.37***	1.68***	35.63**	20.49**	28.84**	20.98***
	(.30)	(.32)	(6.14)	(6.24)	(3.66)	(3.96)
Immigrant Generation's Educational Selectivity (Net Difference Index: Education of Immigrants and Source Populations)		1.54**		34.00***		17.65**
		(.43)		(8.39)		(5.32)
Constant	12.13***	11.60***	47.19***	35.53***	73.62***	67.57***
	(.16)	(.20)	(3.20)	(3.88)	(2.00)	(2.46)
R-squared	0.67	.77	.53	.70	0.67	.76

+p<.10, * p<.05, ** p<.01, ***p<.001
Source: IPUMS 1990

36% more college educated persons and 29% more high school graduates among the 1.5 generation than those with the lowest immigrant socioeconomic status.

The second models in Table 5.3 add immigrants' educational selectivity to the equation. In all cases, this addition increases the explained variance (R^2) and decreases the coefficients of immigrant socioeconomic status. For example, including educational selectivity in the model explains over ¾ of the variance in mean years of schooling among the 1.5-generation groups. The decline in the coefficients of immigrant socioeconomic status in Model 2 indicates that part of the influence of socioeconomic status on average group educational outcomes is actually due to its correlation with immigrants' selectivity. In fact, selectivity is a significant predictor of all three educational outcomes among the 1.5-generation groups. For example, a one unit increase in the NDI corresponds to 1.54 additional average years of schooling, controlling for average socioeconomic status. The most positively selected group also has almost 24% more college educated persons and almost 18% more high school graduates. Interestingly, immigrants' educational selectivity appears to have the strongest effect on the percent college educated; increasing the explained variance from less than 53% to 70%.[4]

Regression Results: The Second Generation

Table 5.4 presents similar regression results, but for second-generation groups. I first add the average socioeconomic status of the group and then the average educational selectivity of the immigrant group. The findings are similar to the results for the 1.5-generation groups: net of average socioeconomic status, immigrants' educational selectivity significantly affects the educational attainment of second-generation national-origin groups. However, there is one exception: when both educational selectivity and socioeconomic status are included in the model predicting percentage of high school graduates, neither are significant. This might be due to the fact that there is less variability in percent high school graduates than other educational attainment outcomes, and less variability among the second generation than the 1.5 generation. In other words; high school graduation might become the norm if a person is born in the U.S. The other difference

Table 5.4. Coefficients of Models of the Determinants of Educational Attainment among 2nd Generation Immigrant Groups in the United States, 1997-2001 (N=32) (standard errors in parentheses)

Independent Variables	Mean Years of Schooling		% Some College		% H.S. Graduates	
	Model 1	Model 2	Model 1	Model 2	Model 1	Model 2
Immigrant Generation's Socioeconomic Status (Occupational Status, Income, Education)	1.75***	1.19***	28.65***	16.32*	11.92*	7.76
	(.35)	(.42)	(6.43)	(7.22)	(4.60)	(5.70)
Immigrant Generation's Educational Selectivity (Net Difference Index: Education of Immigrants and Source Populations)		1.26*		27.68**		9.34
		(.56)		(9.71)		(7.67)
Constant	13.03***	12.60***	59.60***	50.10***	87.22***	84.02***
	(.18)	(.26)	(3.35)	(4.49)	(2.39)	(3.54)
R-squared	.45	.53	.40	.53	.18	.22

+p<.10, * p<.05, ** p<.01, ***p<.001
Source: March CPS 1997-2001

between the two groups is that less of the variance in educational attainment is explained by the variables included in the analysis. For example, 53% of the variance in percent college educated is explained for second-generation groups, compared to 70% for 1.5-generation groups. Similarly, over half of the variability in average years of schooling is explained for the second generation, while over ¾ of the variability is explained for the 1.5-generation groups. This finding most likely reflects the different experiences of the 1.5 and second generation: having grown up entirely in the United States, the second generation may be less influenced by the migration experiences and characteristics of the immigrant generation. In any case, readers should be reminded that the large amount of variance explained is at the group-level of analysis, and would not apply at the individual level. Results at the group level might be stem from ecological fallacy and not apply at the individual level. I thus turn now to additional analyses to examine whether the selectivity findings hold at the individual level.

RESULTS: INDIVIDUAL-LEVEL

Descriptive Results

Having shown that educational selectivity is an important variable affecting group-level differences in educational attainment outcomes among children of immigrants, I now turn to individual-level analyses. I address the question of whether immigrants' educational selectivity contributes to explaining the advantages or disadvantages associated with pan-ethnic group membership for children of immigrants. Specifically, I consider whites (consisting of children of immigrants with national origins in Europe or Canada), blacks (national origins in Haiti, Jamaica), Asians (national origins in Asia), and Latinos (national origins in Latin America or Spanish-speaking Caribbean). I examine two educational transitions that are crucial influences on subsequent labor market outcomes: high school graduation and college attendance.

Table 5.5 shows the means and standard deviations of the variables included in this analysis by race/ethnicity for the 1.5 generation and the second generation. The table shows that there are sharp disparities in educational outcomes among the groups, particularly between Asians and Latinos. Generally, Asians have the highest levels of educational

Table 5.5. Means and Standard Deviations of Variables Included in Individual-Level Analysis by Ethnic/Racial Group, ages 20-40

	White	Black	Asian	Latino
1.5 Generation, 1990 Census				
College Educated	0.62	0.66	0.76	0.40
High School Graduate	0.90	0.88	0.93	0.67
Age	30.03	25.87	26.71	27.97
	(5.82)	(4.52)	(5.57)	(5.69)
Age at Immigration	3.84	6.14	4.38	4.78
	(3.22)	(3.14)	(3.40)	(3.35)
Female	0.48	0.56	0.51	0.51
Central City	0.33	0.55	0.38	0.48
Immigrant Group's				
Socioeconomic Status	0.60	0.46	0.68	0.09
(Occupational Status,				
Income, Education)	(.19)	(.18)	(.15)	(.13)
Immigrant Group's				
Educational Selectivity	.43	.67	.63	.23
(Net Difference Index)	(.16)	(.08)	(.08)	(.19)
N	2058	272	1881	5621
Second Generation, 1997-2001 CPS				
College Educated	0.69	0.75	0.79	0.48
High School Graduate	0.94	0.89	0.98	0.80
Age	30.99	26.37	27.27	28.37
	(6.03)	(4.78)	(5.66)	(5.93)
Female	0.51	0.63	0.51	0.54
Central City	0.24	0.51	0.40	0.40
Immigrant Group's				
Socioeconomic Status	0.50	0.39	0.60	0.07
(Occupational Status,				
Income, Education)	(.25)	(.24)	(.20)	(.12)
Immigrant Group's				
Educational Selectivity	.43	.56	.64	.19
(Net Difference Index)	(.19)	(.21)	(.09)	(.19)
N	1162	65	255	2036

attainment, while Latinos have the lowest. Whites and blacks also have much higher attainment than Latinos, although not as high as Asians. For example, 76% of 1.5-generation Asians have some college schooling, compared to only 40% of 1.5-generation Latinos. One and a half generation whites and blacks have similar levels of educational attainment. Among the second generation, Asians are also the most educated. Second-generation Latinos again have the lowest levels of attainment: only 80% are high school graduates and only 48% have some college education.

The independent variables in this analysis include age, age at migration (for the 1.5 generation), sex, central city of residence, and immigrants' socioeconomic status and educational selectivity, both defined at the level of the national-origin group.[5] The table shows that among both the 1.5 generation and the second generation, blacks are more likely to be female (63% among the second generation), and also more often reside in central cities than the other groups. Whites are the least urban (only 24% of second-generation whites are located in central cities, compared to over half of blacks). As for the immigrant groups' socioeconomic status and selectivity, Latinos tend to come from immigrant groups with the lowest socioeconomic status and with the least positive selectivity, while Asians tend to have higher socioeconomic status and higher selectivity. Blacks and whites fall in between these two groups: whites tend to have high socioeconomic status but are less selective than Asians or blacks, and blacks have lower socioeconomic status than whites or Asians, but have higher selectivity than whites and Latinos.

MULTIVARIATE ANALYSIS

High School Graduation

Tables 5.6 and 5.7 show odds ratios of the determinants of high school graduation among 1.5 and second-generation adults in the United States. The significance levels reflect the use of robust standard errors to correct for the clustering at the level of the immigrant group.[6] Model 1 includes only the broad ethnic/racial groups as predictors of high school graduation, with whites as the comparison group. These results show that for the 1.5 generation (Table 5.6), blacks do not differ significantly from whites in rates of high school completion. Asians,

Table 5.6. Odds Ratios of Models of the Determinants of High School
Graduation among 1.5-Generation Persons aged 20-40 in the United States,
1990

	Model 1	Model 2	Model 3
Black	0.820	1.587	1.004
Asian	1.676*	1.335	1.102
Latino	0.239**	1.335	1.252
Age		1.017+	1.023**
Age at Immigration (approximate)		.962***¹	0.950**
Female		1.239**	1.245**
Central City		.702*	0.738*
Immigrant Group's Socioeconomic Status		33.222*	15.491**
(Occupational Status, Income, Education)			
Immigrant Group's Educational Selectivity			3.885**
(Net Difference Index)			
Observations	9832	9832	9832

Robust standard errors, adjusted for clustering at national-origin
group level:
+p<.10, * p<.05, ** p<.01, ***p<.001
Source: IPUMS 1990

however, are 1.7 times as likely to graduate high school as whites;
Latinos are approximately 75% less likely to graduate high school as
white 1.5-generation adults. Similarly, among the second generation
(Table 5.7), Asians are over two times as likely as whites to graduate
high school, and second-generation Latinos are approximately 75% less
likely to graduate high school than whites.

Model 2 adds individual-level controls to the analysis as well as
the average socioeconomic status of the immigrant group. These
variables generally have results consistent with the literature. Age has
little effect for both 1.5 and second generations, reflecting little

Table 5.7. Odds Ratios of Models of the Determinants of High School Graduation among Second-Generation Persons aged 20-40 in the Unitec States, 1997-2001

	Model	Model 2	Model 3
Black	0.465	0.700	0.581
Asian	2.634**	2.291**	1.886*
Latino	0.247**	0.626*	0.639**
Age		1.020**	1.025**
Female		1.270**	1.291**
Central City		0.671*	0.705**
Immigrant Group's Socioeconomic Status (Occupational Status, Income, Education)		9.042**	4.966**
Immigrant Group's Educational Selectivity (Net Difference Index)			3.143**
Observations	7289	7289	7289

Robust standard errors, adjusted for clustering at national-origin group level:
+p<.10, * p<.05, ** p<.01, ***p<.001
Source: March CPS 1997-2001

variation in age in the sample. Age at migration has a negative effect for the 1.5 generation. In addition, women are slightly more likely to graduate high school than men among both the 1.5 and second generation.

Central city residence has a negative influence on the odds of high school completion for both the 1.5 and second generations. The immigrant group's average socioeconomic status has a large effect: among the 1.5 generation, those from immigrant groups with the highest socioeconomic status are 33 times more likely to graduate high school than those from groups with the lowest socioeconomic status. Among the second generation, those from immigrant groups with the highest socioeconomic status are over nine times as likely to graduate high school as those with the lowest socioeconomic status.

The factors added in Model 2 also change some of the racial/ethnic group membership findings, partly explaining the Asian advantage. Among the 1.5 generation, Asians are still slightly more likely to graduate high school than whites, but the advantage decreases from 1.7 to 1.3 times as likely, and is no longer statistically significant. Among the second generation (Table 5.7), the Asian advantage is also partly explained as the odds ratio declines from 2.6 to 2.3, net of the factors in Model 2. In addition, these factors explain the disadvantage for Latinos among the 1.5 generation; net of these factors, 1.5-generation Latinos do not significantly differ from whites in their likelihood of graduating from high school. For the second generation, adding these controls substantially decreases the Latino disadvantage relative to whites (the odds ratio changes from .247 to .626). Therefore, the lower socioeconomic status of Latino immigrants explains part of the Latino disadvantage in high school graduation rates relative to whites.

Model 3 adds immigrants' educational selectivity to the models in Tables 5.6 and 5.7. Immigrants' educational selectivity is an important predictor of high school graduation: net of other factors for the 1.5 generation; those from immigrant groups with one additional unit increase in educational selectivity are almost four times as likely to graduate high school as those from immigrant groups with the lowest educational selectivity. Among the second generation, an increase in immigrants' educational selectivity corresponds to a nearly five time increase in the likelihood of high school graduation. Adding the immigrant group's educational selectivity in Model 3 also decreases the odds ratio on immigrant group socioeconomic status substantially from 33.22 to 15.49 for the 1.5 generation, and from 9.04 to 4.97 for the second generation. This indicates that part of the influence of immigrant group socioeconomic status is actually due to its correlation with selectivity.

Adding immigrants' educational selectivity partly explains some of the racial/ethnic group findings. Although the Asian 1.5 generation's differences from whites were explained previously, the odds ratio does decline even further. Asian advantage over whites for the second generation is also partly explained, as the odds ratio declines from 2.29 to 1.89.

Table 5.8. Odds Ratios of Models of the Determinants of College
Education among 1.5-Generation Persons aged 20-40 in the
United States, 1990

	Model	Model 2	Model 3
Black	1.202	1.928	1.176
Asian	1.897**	1.765**	1.404
Latino	0.418**	1.434	1.251
Age		1.025*	1.031**
Age at Immigration (approximate)		0.984	0.972*
Female		1.172**	1.177**
Central City		0.931	0.977
Immigrant Group's Socioeconomic Status (Occupational Status, Income, Education)		10.512*	4.047***
Immigrant Group's Educational Selectivity (Net Difference Index)			5.111***
Observations	9832	9832	9832

Robust standard errors, adjusted for clustering at national-
origin group level:
+p<.10, * p<.05, ** p<.01, ***p<.001
Source: IPUMS 1990

College Attendance

Tables 5.8 and 5.9 show odds ratios of the determinants of some
college attainment among 1.5 and second-generation adults in the
United States. Model 1 shows that among the 1.5 generation (Table
5.8), blacks do not differ significantly from whites in the odds of
attending college, while Asians are 1.9 times more likely and Latinos
are less than half as likely to attend college as whites. Among the
second generation (Table 5.9), Asians are over two times as likely to
attend college as whites, while Latinos are much less likely to do so.

Table 5.9. Odds Ratios of Models of the Determinants of College Education among Second-Generation Persons aged 20-40 in the United States, 1997-2001

	Model 1	Model 2	Model 3
Black	0.903	1.086	0.887
Asian	2.035**	1.841*	1.530+
Latino	0.391***	0.677*	0.671**
Age		1.003	1.007
Female		1.348***	1.369**
Central City		0.920	0.957
Immigrant Group's Socioeconomic Status (Occupational Status, Income, Education)		3.618***	1.904+
Immigrant Group's Educational Selectivity (Net Difference Index)			3.221**
Observations	7289	7289	7289

Robust standard errors, adjusted for clustering at national-origin group level:
+p<.10, * p<.05, ** p<.01, ***p<.001
Source: March CPS 1997-2001

Model 2 adds individual-level controls to the analysis as well as the average socioeconomic status of the immigrant group. For both the Asian 1.5 and second generations, part of their advantage over whites is explained by these factors, the most important of which is the higher socioeconomic status of the immigrant generation. For example, among the second generation, the odds ratio for Asians declines from 2.0 to 1.8 once these variables are added to the equation. Nevertheless, even controlling for these factors, both 1.5 and second-generation Asians are still more likely than whites to attend college. In contrast, the disadvantage of the Latino 1.5 generation, and part of the disadvantage of the second generation, is explained by individual background variables and immigrants' socioeconomic status.

Model 3 introduces immigrants' educational selectivity to the equation. For blacks and Latinos, immigrants' educational selectivity does not change the substantive results. For the Asian 1.5 and second generations, however, immigrants' selectivity is an important factor explaining their advantage in terms of college attendance. Once selectivity is introduced into the model, the odds ratio of Asians attending college decreases from almost 1.8 times as likely as whites, to 1.4 times as likely among the 1.5 generation, which does not significantly differ from whites. Among the second generation, the Asian advantage in terms of college attendance relative to whites is also almost entirely explained by the higher educational selectivity of the immigrant generation.

Summary and Discussion

Aiming to tackle the long-standing question of how to explain ethnic group differences in educational outcomes, this chapter highlights the previously neglected influence of immigrant selectivity. Understanding where immigrants were situated in their home country's system of educational stratification prior to migration can help explain where their children end up in the American educational stratification system. I find that the average educational selectivity of the immigrant group significantly affects the mean years of schooling, percent high school graduates, and percent who have attended college among 1.5 and second-generation children of immigrants at the ethnic group level of analysis. Educational selectivity also explains a substantial portion of the variance in ethnic group differences for these same three outcomes. Even controlling for immigrants' average socioeconomic status, higher educational selectivity among the immigrant generation is associated with higher educational attainment among the next generation. I also show that immigrant selectivity is a significant predictor of educational attainment among immigrants' children at the individual level. Furthermore, immigrant selectivity is an important factor contributing to broad ethnic/racial group differences in educational attainment, especially college attendance rates. In particular, it helps to explain the high college attendance rates among Asians.

Consistent with theories of class reproduction (Bourdieu 1973; Bowles and Gintis 1976; Willis 1977), this chapter suggests that education is not often a vehicle for upward mobility among immigrant groups, but rather serves to reproduce existing stratification systems, including those carried over from other countries. In other words, relative class position, measured by the relative pre-migration educational attainment of the immigrant generation, is being reproduced to some extent among the next generation in the United States. As my findings suggest, when education is conceptualized in a broad sense such that not just the degree attained is considered, the importance of this relative educational attainment, or educational selectivity, becomes clear.

Consistent with theories of ethnic, social and cultural capital, I also find that immigrants' selectivity matters above and beyond the absolute level of schooling, occupational status or income of the immigrant groups, and actually conditions non-economic factors. That is, educational selectivity (as well as educational attainment) may capture less tangible forms of capital that either hinder or facilitate success in school. For example, children in immigrant groups that are highly selective may be expected to attain a certain level of schooling, perhaps comparable to the relative level the immigrants' themselves attained in the home country. My results after controlling for income and occupational status further suggest that selectivity influences non-economic factors that condition educational outcomes. In other words, it is not only economic differences that determine who among the second generation will graduate high school and attend college: some immigrant parents are pushing their children to rise to a higher than average class position, which in turn impels the second generation towards higher educational attainment levels. Indeed, Chapter Four's results support this interpretation, since we saw that youths from highly selective immigrant groups were likely to perceive that their parents had high aspirations for their educational success.

Although the findings of chapter are tentative given data limitations, the results are consistent with the idea that immigrants' educational selectivity matters for the next generation's education, beyond its association with absolute measures of socioeconomic status. The results suggest that stratification models may need to be revised in the case of children of immigrant parents to consider immigrants' pre-migration class position. In the next chapter, I compare the use of immigrants' pre-migration socioeconomic status to the use of immigrants' post-migration socioeconomic status, as the benchmarks from which to understand mobility patterns from one generation to the next, to illustrate how assimilation trajectories vary for several immigrant groups.

NOTES

[1] Borjas (1993) found that earnings of second-generation workers are more heavily influenced by the earnings of their parents' generation than by the earnings of current immigrants from the same source country. To this end, I followed Borjas's method of using younger aged children of immigrants (ages 20-40), and earlier data from the immigrant generation, to ensure that there was overlap of parents and children in the analysis.

[2] I included only adults ages 20-40 so that they are old enough to have at least attended some college, yet young enough to be the children of the immigrant generation.

[3] Since the number of cases is only 32, the model would be highly unstable if I included more than 2-3 predictors. However, I did try the analysis with a number of other possible predictors, none of which were significant: mean age of 1.5 or second generation in sample, country distance from U.S., source country income inequality, and per capita GDP in the source country. Two additional source country characteristics did influence educational attainment among children of immigrants, but only through their effects on immigrants' socioeconomic status and selectivity. The literacy rate, contrary to what one might expect, is negatively related to educational attainment among children of immigrants: children of immigrants from countries with higher literacy rates had lower educational attainment. This counterintuitive finding is entirely explained away by immigrants' selectivity, since immigrants from countries with higher educational attainment levels are more likely to be less positively selected. Those from countries where English is spoken have higher educational attainment, but this is because immigrants from these countries have higher socioeconomic statuses in the United States.

[4] I investigated whether any one national-origin group or groups of countries were driving the results. I ran the regressions excluding each of the 32 countries to examine whether the results would differ if any one country was not included in the sample, and found that the substantive results did not change. I also replicated the regression analyses using only 20 countries (those in the low/low and high/high cells in Table 5.2). Again, educational selectivity was

still significant at the .05 level, net of socioeconomic status, even though the standard errors were larger (results available upon request).

[5] The findings in this section should be treated as tentative given that I cannot control for family background factors, such as parents' educational attainment, which have been found to be important predictors of educational attainment.

[6] I follow a similar method as that employed by Borjas (2001) of using a "mixed" regression model with the dependent variable defined at the individual level, while some of the independent variables are defined at the group level. Since the residuals among the observations within the same national-origin group are correlated, I correct the standard errors to account for the structure of the data using STATA's cluster option in logistic regression models.

CHAPTER 6

Upwards, Downwards, Sideways?
The Assimilation Trajectories of Contemporary Immigrant Groups

Thus far, this book has shown how immigrant selectivity varies by country of origin and shapes educational outcomes among children of immigrants in the United States. This chapter examines the implications of immigrant selection for observed patterns of inter-generational social mobility for immigrant groups. I compare the pre-migration educational distributions of immigrants to the educational distributions of children of immigrants in the United States to assess whether various national-origin groups experience upward or downward mobility, or no mobility at all.

While immigration scholars recognize the tremendous diversity in socioeconomic characteristics among contemporary immigrants, they often neglect the fact that not all immigrants start on the bottom rung of the ladder (Perlmann and Waldinger 1997). Studies that do consider the advantages that certain groups have upon arrival make only passing reference to the fact that these immigrants originated from distinct socioeconomic environments prior to migration, and focus instead on the contexts of reception in the United States (Portes and Rumbaut 1996; Portes and Rumbaut 2001; Portes and Zhou 1993; Zhou 1999; Zhou 2001). In terms of understanding social mobility or socioeconomic assimilation across generations, this neglect is particularly problematic. Often, the benchmark for studies of assimilation is the moment immigrants arrive in the United States, and the second generation is characterized as moving upwards, downwards, or stagnating, compared to the first generation's socioeconomic position attained after arrival in the United States (see, for example, Farley and Alba 2002; Zhou 2001). According to this view, for example, Mexicans are viewed as experiencing substantial upward mobility simply because their parents have very low educational attainments by U.S. standards and the second generation completes more years of schooling than the first generation (Alba and Nee 2003; Farley and Alba 2002).

Other studies characterize immigrants' children as experiencing decline, stagnation, or progress depending upon how their socioeconomic outcomes compare to native-born whites (Hirschman 2001). In these studies, the second generation is assumed to be moving upwards if their outcomes surpass those of native-born whites, and downwards if they are below. But this approach ignores the fact that immigrant generations come from diverse class backgrounds. Thus, two problems may occur: certain second-generation groups may be viewed as experiencing extraordinary upward mobility because their educational outcomes surpass those of native-born whites, and other groups may be seen as experiencing downward mobility because their outcomes are below those of whites (Hirschman 2001). For example, Indians might be viewed as an upwardly mobile group because the second generation surpasses the educational attainments of native-born whites, even though the immigrant generation also surpassed native-born whites. On the other hand, Mexicans might be viewed as downwardly mobile because the educational attainments of the second generation are below those of native-born whites. However, without taking into account the immigrant group's pre-migration socioeconomic status, both accounts of mobility are deficient. Comparing the second generation's outcomes only to the first generation's post-migration status neglects the fact that many immigrant groups experience downward mobility in the United States and were of higher status in the home country. Comparing the second generation's outcomes only to their native-born peers ignores the fact that not all immigrant groups start at the bottom.

This confusion over whether the second generation should be weighed against their parents or their native peers can be resolved by recognizing that second-generation outcomes need to be compared to the first generation to assess progress, but the second generation must also be compared to their native peers to put their outcomes in context (see Chapa 1990). In addition, however, I argue that the first generation's socioeconomic status also needs to be put into the proper context, and should be evaluated based on immigrants' socioeconomic position *prior* to migration. After all, immigrants base decisions about migration not only on whether they will be better off, but whether their children will be better off in the United States. Many immigrants experience downward mobility upon migrating to the United States because their skills and education are not rewarded in the U.S. job market (Zeng and Xie 2004). From this perspective, whether immigrants' socioeconomic status in the United States after migration should be taken as the benchmark from which to study assimilation patterns is questionable.

Second-Generation Decline, Stagnation, or Advancement?

In delineating the different outcomes of the adaptation process, segmented assimilation theory stresses the influences of factors such as governmental policy, type of societal reception, the strength and resources of the ethnic community, and socioeconomic background (Portes and Borocz 1989; Portes and Zhou 1993). This literature has thus tended to focus on "contexts of reception," which can be described as a framing that asks *to what* immigrants assimilate rather than asking *from what* they come.

Empirical tests of the segmented assimilation model view the observation of divergent outcomes among the second generation as support for the theory. For example, Hirschman (2001) argues that the finding that a few groups of immigrant youths have above-average rates of nonenrollment in school, while most others have school enrollment rates similar to those of their native-born peers, supports the segmented assimilation model. Zhou (2001) concludes that nearly all children of immigrants progress beyond their parents, but that Asians progress most rapidly because of their high educational attainment relative to whites and Latino immigrant groups. However, the fact that many Asian groups may not be experiencing true upward mobility, given that their parents may have been elites in their home countries, is not often fully engaged. Studies that ignore the different starting points from which socioeconomic assimilation occurs cannot tell us *in what direction* assimilation is occurring.

Alba and Nee (2003) recognize that not all immigrants begin at the bottom of the socioeconomic queue, and that many bring substantial educational credentials with them. However, they argue that when immigrants, such as those from Mexico or Central America, do actually begin at the bottom of the stratification system in the United States, it is certain that the second generation will experience upward mobility. Likewise, Smith (2003) argues that Mexicans experience upward mobility over generations because each consecutive generation closes the education gap with native whites. Other scholars conclude that the dramatic increase in educational attainment from the first to the second generation is a clear sign of intergenerational progress (Chavez 1991; Grogger and Trejo 2002; McCarthy and Valdez 1985).

Focusing on employment patterns, Waldinger and Feliciano (2004) also find little support for the notion of "downward assimilation" among second-generation Mexicans. While they note that there is a "downward" tendency in terms of employment rates and hours for the second as compared to the first generation, employment patterns for the Mexican second generation are much better than for blacks or Puerto Ricans and compare favorably with those of native whites (Waldinger and Feliciano 2004). These studies, which compare the second generation to the first generation, contend that the segmented assimilation theory's "downward assimilation" path is overstated, at least as applied to the Mexican case.

No studies of the second generation consider that the first generation's socioeconomic position in the United States might not be the appropriate benchmark to understand assimilation patterns. Thus, instead of asking which factors might facilitate or impede upward, downward or stagnant mobility, this paper addresses the assumptions of segmented assimilation theory and examines the observed assimilation patterns of some major immigrant groups to the United States using two different possible benchmarks. The first of these uses the immigrant generation's educational attainment relative to U.S. natives (post-migration), and the second uses this attainment relative to the population in the home country (pre-migration).

DATA AND METHODS

To analyze educational attainment among second-generation immigrant groups in the United States, this chapter uses the Current Population

Survey Data, as described in Chapter Five. Here, to simplify the presentation of results, I examined only 17 immigrant groups out of the original 32, corresponding to the 17 groups with sample sizes of at least 100 second-generation persons ages 20-40 in the survey. As in the previous chapter, I included only 20-40 year olds so that the second generation are old enough to have completed much of their education, but young enough to be the children of the immigrant generation. The countries of origin that fit these criteria are Canada, China, Colombia, Cuba, Dominican Republic, El Salvador, Greece, India, Ireland, Italy, Japan, Mexico, Netherlands, Philippines, Poland, Portugal, and Puerto Rico.

To examine the relative starting points of the immigrant generation, I calculated net difference indexes (NDI) to compare immigrants' educational attainments with nonmigrants in the homeland or U.S. natives, adjusted for age, along all points of the education distribution (see Chapter Three for a detailed discussion of the data collection and NDI calculations). In interpreting the NDIs, the reader should keep in mind that the higher the NDI, the more educated the immigrants are relative to the comparison group, and if immigrants are more often less educated than the comparison group, the value of NDI will be negative. I calculated net difference indexes that compare the educational attainments of immigrants to similarly aged U.S. natives, and that compare immigrants to similarly aged nonmigrants in the home country. In addition, I created an NDI to compare 20-40 year old second-generation adults to similarly-aged U.S. natives of native parentage (the 3rd+ generation).

Using measures of educational attainment relative to a comparison group, calculated by the NDIs, allows me to account for changes in educational distributions over time, and the fact that all populations are generally becoming more educated over time. Not accounting for this fact may lead to incorrect conclusions about social mobility: the younger generation is likely to be more educated than the previous generation due to general population trends, yet this is not necessarily an indication of upward mobility.

In this chapter, I first examine assimilation patterns of 17 immigrant groups by comparing second-generation educational attainments to the immigrant generation's educational attainments, both relative to U.S. natives. This analysis is comparable to most studies of assimilation: immigrants' socioeconomic status (here, only educational attainment) in the United States context is taken as the benchmark from which to discern adaptation patterns of the next generation (see Alba and Nee 2003; Farley and Alba 2002). Second, I consider the alternative benchmark of the immigrants' relative educational position prior to migration. In this case, I again compare second-generation educational attainments to U.S. natives. However, for the immigrant generation, I compare educational attainments to those of the nonmigrant population in their home country. I do not include any additional control variables because my concern is with observable outcomes rather than outcomes holding other factors constant (see Perlmann 2001 for a similar approach).

RESULTS

Assimilation From What? Immigrants' Educational Attainments Relative to U.S. Natives

To examine how the educational attainments of various second-generation immigrant groups compare to the immigrant generation, Figure 6.1 frames the data in a variety of ways. First, each point on the graph represents the NDI of that group relative to U.S. natives (in the case of the second generation, the comparison group is U.S. natives of native parentage). Second, the net difference index for the second generation is compared to the NDI for the immigrant generation to assess whether there is upward, downward, or no mobility. The NDI for the first generation is on the left, connected by a line to the NDI for the second generation. Third, net difference indexes for each group are calculated separately for males and females to assess whether there are gender differences in assimilation trajectories. As mentioned earlier, the NDI is preferable to absolute measures of educational attainment (such as years of schooling completed or degrees attained) because it accounts for the fact that educational attainments in general have increased over time in the United States and throughout the world. Thus, the first generation (who are older), would almost always be less educated than the second generation, just based on general societal changes; whether this should be considered upward mobility is debatable, since it does not necessarily mean that the second generation are better off in relative terms. Figure 6.1 illustrates the tremendous

Figure 6.1. Relative Educational Distributions of 17 Immigrant Groups, 1st and 2nd Generations (1st Generation Relative to U.S. Natives)

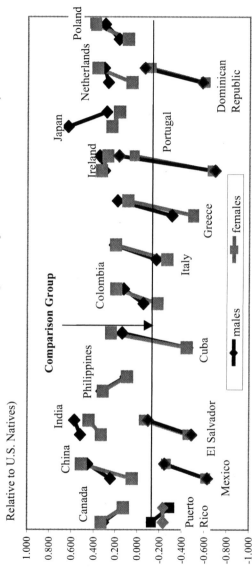

Notes: The Net Difference Indexes are shown for the first generation on the left, and the second generation on the right. The reference group for the first generation are all U.S. Natives of the same age range; the reference group for the second generation are all U.S. Natives of Native parentage of the same age range. The data for the second generation are from the 1998-2002 CPS; the data for the first generation are from the 1970 and 1980 U.S. Censuses.

125

variability in human capital that different immigrant groups have relative to U.S. natives. It is clear from the graph that the immigrant groups are all beginning at different educational levels relative to U.S. natives. Eight of the 17 first-generation groups have educational distributions which surpass those of U.S. natives overall (Canada, China, India, Philippines, Ireland, Japan, Netherlands, Poland); among those, Indian and Japanese males stand out as having the highest relative educational attainments. The NDI indicates that a Japanese males' educational attainment will exceed that of a U.S. native 64% more often than the reverse is true, while Indian males' educational attainment will exceed that of a U.S. native 52% more often. At the other end of the spectrum, nine of the 17 first-generation groups, and Portuguese, Mexican, and Dominican immigrants in particular, are less educated than U.S. natives. For example, the Portuguese NDI of -.67 indicates that 67% of the time, a U.S. native would be more educated than a Portuguese immigrant.

In contrast, most of the second-generation groups (13 of 17) have higher educational attainments than their U.S. native counterparts, with the exception of Puerto Ricans, Salvadorans, Dominicans, and Mexicans. These results are generally consistent with those of Hirschman (2001) who, focusing on 15-17 year olds, found that second-generation youths often exceed their native peers in educational enrollment, with a few exceptions. Hirschman concluded that his findings lend some support to the "immigrant optimism" thesis that members of the second generation exceed natives because their parents are especially optimistic and motivated (Kao and Tienda 1995). However, he also concludes that the segmented assimilation theory is correct in pointing out that not all groups experience substantial upward mobility.

Nevertheless, with the exception of Puerto Ricans, all of the groups with lower than average educational attainments among the first generation could be considered as experiencing upward mobility by the second generation. Thus, for example, even though the educational attainment of the Mexican second generation is quite low relative to natives (NDI=-.25 for males and females), the Mexican immigrant generation was far less educated relative to U.S. natives (-.63). This picture makes it clear that, at least when U.S. natives are the comparison group, Mexicans, Salvadorans, Cubans, Colombians, Italians, Greeks, Portuguese, and Dominicans all appear to follow the "straight-line" assimilation path; that is, the groups start out below U.S. natives in educational attainment, and over the course of one generation, either reduce the gap (in the Mexican, Salvadoran, and Dominican cases), or eliminate it completely to surpass U.S. natives (in the Cuban, Colombian, Italian, Greek and Portuguese cases). These patterns do not differ substantially by gender for these groups.

Among the immigrant groups who initially started with higher than average educational attainments, Canadians, Filipinos, Irish females, and Japanese move towards convergence (in a downward direction) with U.S. natives in the second generation. In the case of Japanese males, whose immigrant generation begins substantially more educated than U.S. natives, the assimilation trajectory in a downward direction towards convergence with U.S. native males is particularly apparent. Still, all of these groups' second generations continue to surpass U.S. natives in educational attainment. The second generations from India, the Netherlands, China, Poland, and males from Ireland improve on the high position of their parents to achieve even greater educational attainment relative to U.S. natives. For these groups, there is clear upward mobility, to a level that far surpasses the U.S. norm. However, we do see some gender differences. In the Chinese case, we see that most of the substantial upward mobility for the group overall comes from the female second generation, who significantly advance beyond from their mothers' position, which was slightly above the norm for U.S. female natives. Second-generation male Chinese also improve relative to their fathers, but the immigrant males begin at a higher position than females, which lessens the increase. In the Indian case, the advantage held by immigrant males is continued into the second generation, although both males and females exhibit substantial upward mobility. In the Irish case, as mentioned earlier, females move towards convergence with U.S. native females, while males move in an upward direction.

The pattern for Puerto Ricans belies all these groups. Both first-generation males and females have lower educational distributions than their U.S. native counterparts (although their educational attainments are not nearly as far below natives as are some other groups, such as Mexicans or Dominicans), but the pattern diverges for males and females. Females do not make any progress over the first generation, and maintain the same low relative educational attainment level in the second generation. The males, on the other hand, experience downward assimilation. The second-generation Puerto Rican males are doing even worse relative to U.S. natives than their first-generation fathers, whose relative educational distribution was only slightly below that of U.S. native men. This case of downward mobility is consistent with the "downward assimilation" path of the segmented assimilation model.

Assimilation From What? Immigrants' Relative Pre-Migration Educational Attainment

The above analysis illustrates the patterns of assimilation when first-generation attainments relative to U.S. natives are used as the initial point of reference. But is this the appropriate benchmark? The first generation were adults when they migrated, so most of their education was completed in the home country, and in that context many of them have excelled beyond average attainment levels. However, the same absolute level of education completed in the homeland may correspond to a much lower position in the U.S. stratification system. Further, many may have experienced downward mobility immediately upon migrating to the United States because they could not translate their educational attainments into occupational outcomes due to language and skill transfer issues. For these reasons, I argue that examining wages, occupational statuses, or educational attainment relative to U.S. natives are not appropriate benchmarks for understanding assimilation trajectories. Since immigrants evaluate their position in the sending country to decide whether they or their children will be better off in the United States, many may decide to migrate despite the prospect that they themselves will lose socioeconomic status if they expect substantial upward mobility for their children.

Figure 6.2 illustrates the assimilation patterns of these immigrant groups when the benchmark becomes the educational distributions of immigrants relative to the populations in their home countries. Immediately apparent is that, in contrast to the previous figure, the originating positions of the various immigrant groups are not as varied. In fact, only Puerto Ricans begin at a position that is below that of nonmigrants in the home country while all of the other immigrant groups are positively selected. Still, the degree to which this is true varies tremendously, with Indian males being the most positively selected group: 98% of the time, they will be more educated than a male in India. In contrast, Mexican males, although more educated

Figure 6.2. Relative Educational Distributions of 17 Immigrant Groups, 1st and 2nd Generations (1st Generation Relative to Home Country Populations)

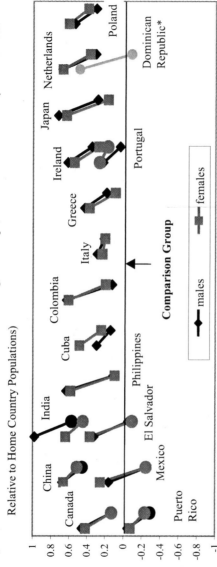

Notes: The Net Difference Indexes are shown for the first generation on the left, and the second generation on the right. The reference group for the first generation is the population in the home country of the same age; the reference group for the second generation are all U.S. Natives of native parentage in the same age range. The data for the second generation are from the 1998-2002 March CPS; the data for the first generation are from the 1970 and 1980 U.S. Censuses.

* Data were not available by gender.

overall than Mexican males that remain in Mexico, are only more educated 16% of the time.

With immigrants' relative pre-migration educational attainments as the benchmark, all of the groups are assimilating in a downward direction. None of the second-generation groups is more relatively educated than their parents' generation. A large part of this downward finding is due to the fact that many of these immigrants are from countries with low overall educational attainments: in the U.S. context, where there are more educational opportunities, and educational distributions are higher overall, it is unlikely the children's educational attainments would be as high relative to U.S. natives as their parents were relative to their homeland populations. Nevertheless, even immigrants from Canada, where educational opportunities are similar to those in the U.S., are highly educated relative to other Canadians. Thus, the patterns reflect something about the migration process itself, and show that migration is a selective process, an option only for those whose resources surpass those of their average countrymen. Yet, to assume that these patterns prove downward assimilation would be misleading as most of these groups' second generations still surpass their native peers in educational attainment. Rather, it appears that a process of convergence with natives is occurring over generations. Nearly all of the second-generation groups' educational attainments are more similar to U.S. natives than the immigrant generation's educational attainments were to their home country counterparts.

However, there are four major exceptions to this convergence: assimilation trajectories of immigrants from Puerto Rico, Mexico, El Salvador, and Dominican Republic are not only in a downward direction, but describe second-generation attainments that are well below their U.S. native peers. From a perspective that considers their parents' above-average educational attainments in their home country, the assimilation patterns of Mexicans, Salvadorans, and Dominicans are especially troubling. These findings suggest that conditions in the U.S. for them or their parents are such that they are, indeed, experiencing downward mobility. In the Puerto Rican case, perhaps the negative selection of migrants combined with the contexts in which second-generation boys and girls grow up may lead to a further downward slide.

The Mexican, Salvadoran, and Dominican cases are important because they illustrate that the interpretations of their assimilation patterns directly hinge on which benchmark is used. Socioeconomic assimilation patterns are completely contradictory depending upon which reference group for the immigrant generation is considered. If the reference group is U.S. natives, then the second generation clearly experiences upward mobility relative to their parents, whose educational attainments fall far below the norm for U.S. natives. However, if the reference group is the immigrants' home country counterparts, part of the actual context in which the adult immigrants received their education, then the second generation is experiencing clear downward mobility. These immigrants were relatively highly educated in their home countries, and the second generation achieves relatively low educational attainments in the U.S. context where they are raised.

Summary and Conclusion

This chapter problematizes the question of assimilation *from what* by showing how the point of reference that is considered as the starting point for assimilation trajectories has important implications for the mobility patterns observed from the first to the second generation.

When compared either to their home countries' populations or U.S. natives, there are some groups whose immigrant generation begins at above-average educational levels. For some of these groups, such as the Filipinos and Canadians, the results are similar regardless of the benchmark used: the second generation assimilates in a downward direction. However, in these cases, the downward trend is not necessarily problematic since it implies an inevitable pattern of convergence to the norm, and these groups' second generations still have above-average educational distributions. Other immigrant groups, such as Indians and Chinese, are very highly selective: they have above-average educational distributions relative to U.S. natives, and educational attainments that are even higher above the average of their home countries' populations. For these groups, the benchmark used to assess assimilation trajectories is somewhat important. The second generation is able to improve on the first generation's educational levels relative to U.S. natives, but do worse than the first generation did relative to their home country's populations. Again, however, the downward trend is not necessarily problematic since these groups' second generations still out-perform their U.S. native counterparts.

For other groups, however, such as Mexicans, Salvadorans, and Dominicans, the choice of the comparison group for the immigrant generation can drastically change the interpretation of assimilation patterns. That is, for these groups, if immigrants' educational position relative to U.S. natives is viewed as the benchmark, all of these groups' second generations advance over the first generation. However, if immigrants' educational position relative to nonmigrants in their homelands is seen as the benchmark, all of these groups experience downward mobility, since the immigrants are positively selected from their home countries. In these cases, the downward pattern is troubling because all of these second-generation groups are doing worse educationally relative to their native peers.

As first noted in Chapter Three, the Puerto Rican case is unique in that it is the only immigrant group that is negatively selected, that is, less educated than the homeland population. In addition, here we see that it is also the only group that does not improve upon the immigrant generation's relative educational position by any measure. If immigrants' home population is used as the benchmark, both male and female second-generation Puerto Ricans do worse than the first generation. However, if the benchmark is immigrants vs. U. S. natives, females remain at a low level, while males slide further downward. In either case, the assimilation prospects of Puerto Ricans are especially dismal, and the patterns for males suggest that Puerto Rican men may be especially vulnerable to downward mobility.

These patterns support the segmented assimilation theory in that they illustrate different outcomes and paths: some immigrant groups are indeed moving ahead, while others are moving behind. For example, the downward assimilation route described by the segmented assimilation model seems to be followed by Puerto Ricans. However, the findings here also illustrate two common paths that are not addressed in segmented assimilation theory. Because immigrant groups often start from a very high relative position, the next generation may either (1) continue to exhibit extraordinary achievement, or (2) may move towards converge with their U.S. native peers.

I argue that immigrants' pre-migration socioeconomic status is the better point of reference to assess assimilation patterns for several reasons. First, the regression analyses in Chapter Five indicated that immigrants' relative pre-migration educational attainment is a much stronger predictor of second-generation educational outcomes than immigrants' post-migration socioeconomic status. Beyond the empirical results, however, there are theoretical reasons for using pre-migration status as the benchmark. The first reason, stressed throughout this book, is that the context in which education is attained, or how that attainment compares to others, is important. Neglecting pre-migration relative educational attainment assumes that a high school degree earned in one context has the same meaning as a high school degree earned in another context. In turn, immigrants who do not have high educational credentials by American standards may, in fact, be quite selective relative to the general home country population because educational opportunities and distributions vary greatly by country (Lieberson 1980).

Second, as Chiswick (1978) first noted, the same number of years of schooling might not convert to the same amount of earnings for immigrants as for native-born Americans because of the "international transferability of skills." More recently, Zeng and Xie (2004) find that place of education plays an important role in determining earnings for Asians in U.S., and they argue that foreign education is valued less highly than U.S. education in the U.S. job market. Therefore, it is reasonable to conclude that many immigrants may experience downward mobility upon migrating to the United States, not only in terms of occupations and earnings, but also in terms of the relative status their educations garnered them in their homelands.

Third, a given number of years of schooling for immigrant parents might not have the same influence on their children as that same number of years of schooling of native parents. This may be true not only because they learn different skills, but also because levels of schooling achieved in different contexts may capture different resources and characteristics. Grogger and Smith (2002) find that there is a weaker link between parental education and children's high school graduation among Mexican immigrants than among U.S. natives. In light of selectivity, this may occur because the immigrant parent's education was obtained in a different context than the United States, a context which is not captured by an absolute measure of educational attainment. In other words, it may take the same amount of drive, tenacity, and perseverance to achieve a high school degree in Mexico as it takes to achieve a college degree in the United States, but without being able to measure the differential between the two contexts in absolute outcomes, researchers miss relevant and enlightening information.

The assimilation patterns presented here suggest that it is just as important to consider assimilation *from what* as it is to consider assimilation *to what*. That the children of many recent immigrants from Asia and Europe are doing well in comparison to U.S. natives is obvious: without exception, all of the Asian and European groups considered here surpass U.S. natives in their overall educational distributions. However, it would be misleading to conclude that all Asian and European groups experience substantial upward mobility. Rather, most of these groups were of relatively high status prior to migrating to the United States; that their children are also doing relatively well should be viewed as a reproduction of their stratification position, rather than upward mobility. That other second-generation groups are not doing as well is also obvious. Children of Mexican, Salvadoran and Dominican migrants are relatively worse off than U.S. natives. While some conclude that this should still be seen as a sign of upward mobility because the immigrants begin at such a low level relative to U.S. natives, I argue that these patterns should not be viewed so optimistically. From the point of view of these groups' first generation, who were of higher educational status than the average person in their homeland, the fact that the second generation's educational levels are below those of U.S. natives is indeed disturbing, especially considered in conjunction with the studies which show little progress from the second to the third generation among Mexican-Americans (Bean et al. 1994; Grogger and Trejo 2002; Livingston and Kahn 2002). Perhaps most troubling is the Puerto Rican case, whose direction of change cannot be viewed optimistically from any point of view. These findings suggest that future research should focus on the factors that not only hinder upward progress, but also facilitate downward trajectories, particularly among immigrant groups of Latin American or Caribbean origin.

CHAPTER 7

Conclusion: Unequal Origins, Unequal Outcomes

Immigration is currently transforming the American social landscape to a greater degree, perhaps, than at any other time in history. While the impact of current immigration remains to be seen, scholars agree that in the long term, the successful adaptation of children of immigrants raised in the United States is crucial. However, as the new second generation comes of age, researchers have observed clear ethnic disparities in educational outcomes that are not explained by family background differences (Feliciano 2001, Portes and Rumbaut 2001, Rumbaut 1997, Steinberg, Brown and Dornbusch 1996), and which, in some cases, threaten potential success. Such divergent outcomes have led scholars to formulate theories to explain why some immigrant groups' children seem to follow an upwardly mobile path, while others seem destined to remain in permanent poverty (Portes and Zhou 1993). Segmented assimilation theory argues that individual factors such as parents' human capital, as well as contextual factors, such as government reception, racial prejudices of the receiving society, strengths of the existing ethnic community, and economic conditions (all captured under the umbrella term "modes of incorporation") interact to explain divergent outcomes (Portes and Borocz 1989, Portes and Zhou 1993, Zhou 1999). While in agreement that these factors are important, I argue that an often-neglected factor—the selective nature of immigrants' migration—also helps explain striking educational disparities among immigrants' children, and should be considered within the segmented assimilation viewpoint. Immigration scholars agree that migrants are not random samples of the populations from which they originated (Borjas 1987, 1999), but they disagree considerably about how immigrants are selected and the impact of selective migration on inequality in the United States. This study systematically analyzes immigrant selectivity and its effects on educational inequality.

This research makes two main contributions to the study of immigration and immigrant adaptation. First, I emphasize group-level factors, adding to Portes and Rumbaut's (1996) emphasis on modes of incorporation and group processes, by explicitly including group-level variables in the models predicting educational success. While group-level processes, such as "modes of incorporation," are often implicated when researchers continue to find a significant effect of ethnicity or national-origin on educational outcomes after controlling for individual factors, few studies actually explicitly include group-level variables.

Second, I explicitly examine immigrants' educational selectivity. For any given country that sends immigrants to the United States, including Mexico, the vast majority of the population does *not* migrate, despite the fact that, on the face of it, the economic incentives to do so are obvious. Thus, the migration process itself is inherently unequal, in that only select portions of the home countries' populations either choose to or are able to migrate. Beyond recognizing that the select few who do migrate must differ from those who do not migrate (for examples, see Rumbaut 1997, 1999), little research has been devoted to exploring selectivity and its impact on eventual adaptation in the United States (see Gans 2000, Rumbaut 1999 for discussions of this gap in the literature). Part of the difficulty lies in measuring the concept of selectivity itself. Understanding immigrants' selection adequately requires data on both the sending and receiving sides of the migration process. Most datasets only include data on immigrants once they have arrived in the United States. Some scholars include data on immigrants' pre-migration status but they do not have data on those remaining in the homeland in order to situate those characteristics within a meaningful context (Gonzalez 2002, Rumbaut 1997). Only a few case studies have had comparable data on nonmigrants in the home country (Landale et al 2000; Melendez 1994; Ortiz 1986; Ramos 1992). In contrast to these studies, in this research I create measures of immigrants' educational selectivity from published Census data from 32 sending countries and

U.S. Census on immigrants, and use data from the Census, Current Population Survey, and Children of Immigrants' Longitudinal Study to show that at both the group and individual levels, immigrant groups' educational selectivity contributes to explaining differences in educational outcomes among second-generation youths.

Variability in Immigrant Selectivity

This study's findings run contrary to the common assumption that many immigrants are negatively selected. In fact, nearly all immigrants, with the critical exception of Puerto Ricans, are more educated than the populations in their home countries, although Asian immigrants are more highly selected than Latin American immigrants. Furthermore, there is limited support for the idea that earlier waves of Mexican immigrants are more positively selected than later waves. This research challenges theoretical frameworks based on case studies of Puerto Rico by showing that the finding that Puerto Rican migrants are less educated than their homeland population cannot be generalized to any other immigrant group, all of whom face much greater barriers to entry to the United States. The findings also run contrary to the argument that changing national origins has resulted in immigrants of "declining quality," by showing that more recent immigrants (mainly from Latin America and Asia) actually tend to be more highly selected than those who arrived in the 1960's (mostly from Europe).

The Consequences of Immigrant Selectivity

This study finds that differences in immigrant group selectivity influence second-generation adolescents' educational expectations and aspirations, as well as their perceptions of their parents' aspirations, even controlling for their parents' socioeconomic status and other family background factors. Further, the effect of parents' socioeconomic status in the United States depends upon the average educational selectivity of the immigrant group to which they belong: parents' socioeconomic status has little influence on children's expectations if they belong to a highly select immigrant group, but a strong influence if they belong to a less selective group. These findings support the literature that emphasizes group-level factors by showing that the selection of the immigrant group matters beyond the influence of the family alone.

Selectivity not only affects educational ambitions, but actual educational attainments as well. As immigrants' educational selectivity and average socioeconomic status increases, the educational attainment of second-generation adults also increases, at both the group and individual levels. While they are correlated, both immigrant group's selectivity and socioeconomic status influence the next generation's educational attainment. At the group level, immigrant groups' average socioeconomic status and average educational selectivity together account for well over half of the variance in the percent who are college educated among the 32 one and a half and second-generation groups. Further, at the individual level, the more positive selection of Asian immigrant groups helps explain their second generations' superior high school graduation rates, average years of schooling, and college attendance rates as compared to Europeans, Afro-Caribbeans, or Latin Americans. These results suggest that ethnic educational disparities among the second generation may result from a process of class reproduction. In conjunction with the study's findings on adolescent expectations and aspirations, this suggests that a structural characteristic (selectivity) influences educational attainment because it shapes cultural attributes, such as goals and expectations. These findings challenge explanations for ethnic group differences in educational success that favor cultural influences. For example, although some scholars privilege "oppositional cultures" developed in the U.S. as an explanation for ethnic group differences (Ogbu 1991), this research suggests that a *pre-migration* structural characteristic of immigrant groups important. Furthermore, this study counters arguments that certain national groups intrinsically value education more than others by showing the selection process that is occurring: only select segments of any home country's population comes to the United States, and they are not necessarily representative of their national cultures. While this does not mean that cultural factors are irrelevant, it does suggest that cultural differences may ultimately stem from differences in pre-migration structural positions. Thus, rather than placing a higher value on education than others, some immigrant groups have a higher pre-migration status than their countrymen, an inequality which is reproduced among the next generation in the United States.

Assimilation *From* What?

Examining immigrant selectivity provides a way of understanding where those who migrated to the United States were situated in their home countries' stratification systems prior to migration. If this relative pre-migration class position is considered as the point of reference to understand assimilation patterns, rather than immigrants' post-migration status in the United States, the interpretation of second-generation mobility patterns can be quite different. This study suggests that some groups, such as Mexicans, Salvadorans, and Dominicans, may be experiencing downward mobility if the benchmark is pre-migration status, but upward mobility when it is post-migration status. Puerto Ricans are uniquely disadvantaged, not only in that they are the only migrants that are negatively selected, but also because theirs is the only second-generation group to do worse educationally than the first generation regardless of the point of reference used.

The findings support segmented assimilation theory by showing the divergent outcomes and paths of adaptation for different immigrant groups. However, the study also reveals additional paths not considered by segmented assimilation theory. Namely, that some immigrant groups start from a very high relative class position and the second generation may either maintain that high status or move towards convergence (in a downward direction) with U.S. natives. Simply because some second-generation Asian and European groups surpass U.S. natives in educational attainment does not necessarily mean that they are upwardly mobile. In many cases, the high pre-migration status of the immigrant generation is simply being reproduced among the next generation in the United States context.

Future Research

Immigration currently continues from many of the countries studied, and, even as of the mid 2000's, the second-generation children from many of the immigrant groups studied are still very young. For several of the groups, such as Mexicans, Vietnamese, and Filipinos, the second generation, those born in the United States of immigrant parents, average less than twenty years old as of the year 2000. For Mexicans, the largest immigrant group, a substantial portion of the second generation may be included in the study, but their experiences still might not mirror those of children of the most recent immigrants. For other groups, such as the Vietnamese, the children of immigrants born in the United States included in this study are only a small proportion of their second generation, due to the recent timing of their migration. Only future research as these children come of age will be able to tell us whether the findings of this study apply for all members of the groups, or only for the children of earlier waves of migrants from each country.

Some of the most interesting findings in the study concern the strong impact of educational selectivity on children of immigrants' college ambitions (Chapter Four) and college attendance (Chapter Five). Clearly, in contemporary U.S. society, attending and succeeding in college are crucial to eventual economic success, and the findings suggest that immigrants' selection may have its strongest impact on these outcomes. Unfortunately, due to data limitations, the analyses in this book fall short of truly understanding the second generation's success in college since I was unable to examine the type of college attended or college graduation rates. Future research should investigate how immigrant selection impacts not only how the transition to college is made, but also who attends and graduates from what type of school.

This study also only barely addresses the complex reasons why immigrants are selected as they are from different countries. Distance was one of the predictors of high positive immigrant selection, while refugee status, percent who migrated before 1965, and home country inequality had insignificant effects. Thus, migrants from Asia tended to be much more highly selected than those from Latin America. In addition to the higher psychological and material costs of migration from a more distant origin country, there are likely to be a number of reasons why migrants from Asia tend to be more highly selected than those from Latin America. A complex array of factors, including U.S. immigration policy, the historical relationship between the United States and the origin country, and conditions in the sending country would all influence how and why the U.S. gets a select group of migrants from any particular country. For example, after World War II, economic conditions in Mexico, as well as U.S. policy that recruited unskilled workers under the Bracero program, led to a certain class of Mexican workers migrating to the United States. This historical fact has undoubtedly contributed to the current selection of Mexican immigrants, as migration spawned by social networks continues to this day. Further, my findings from the Mexican case show that the positive selection of Mexican migrants has declined over time, such that the most recent migrants are not much more educated, if at all, than Mexican nonmigrants. Further research is needed on how and why immigrant selection changes over time. In particular, in-depth case studies on specific countries' histories would help to illuminate the selection processes at work.

While immigrants' educational selectivity is likely to be the most important form of selection shaping educational outcomes among the second generation, it is still only one form among many. Immigrants are selected on many additional things, such as occupational status and health, including less tangible, characteristics, such as ambition, appetite for adventure, and motivation. These forms of selection may not necessarily correspond to one another. For example, even immigrants who are among the least educated may be, mentally and physically, among the healthiest from their countries, able to withstand both the physical and mental pressures of the migration process. Indeed, some studies have investigated whether immigrant selection may help explain the "epidemiological paradox" among immigrants— that even low socioeconomic status immigrants tend to have better health outcomes than U.S. natives (Rumbaut and Weeks 1996, Weeks et al 1999). In the case of Puerto Ricans, where I have found that migrants are negatively selected with respect to education, one study's findings suggest that Puerto Rican migrants are positively selected with respect to maternal health attributes (Landale et al 2000).

Future research should also be directed towards understanding exactly what educational selectivity is actually capturing and what the mechanisms are through which it matters for the educational adaptation of immigrants' children. Educational selectivity clearly provides some measure of the prior standing of immigrants in their home countries' educational distributions, or how educated immigrants were relative to others in that country. However, whether that corresponds to immigrants' actual prior relative *social* status is an empirical question. I assume that the two are highly correlated, but in countries where status depends more on other factors, such as political capital, than educational credentials, educational selectivity may not be an appropriate proxy for social status. In some cases, educational selectivity may reflect the greater motivation or ambition of immigrants. My preliminary findings suggest that highly educationally selected immigrant groups have higher educational aspirations and expectations for the next generation, but determining whether that is because they expect their social status to be replicated in the United States, because they have greater social or cultural capital, or because they are simply more ambitious would require more in-depth qualitative investigation.

The findings in the book also suggest that future research should examine how selectivity interacts with other factors, such as discrimination and racial prejudice, in influencing school success for second-generation youths. While Asian success is largely explained by their high immigrant selectivity, I find that the black second generation does not do as well in school as would be predicted by the high selectivity of Haitian and Jamaican immigrants. While selectivity works in the same direction for the black second generation as for Asians, in this case it means that blacks would be doing far worse if not for their high selectivity, not that selectivity explains extraordinary achievement. Partly, this is because the high selectivity of black immigrant groups does not correspond to high socioeconomic status in the United States; it does not translate to high incomes or occupational status as it does for many other immigrant groups. This finding may reflect the harsh reality of racial discrimination that many first-generation black immigrants face. In addition, for black immigrants' children in particular, Americanization may undermine the positive benefits of their immigrant groups' high selectivity, as black youths become disillusioned when faced with the discriminatory nature of U.S. society (Waters 2001).

These suggestions for future research likely just touch on the numerous possibilities for expanding on the topics of immigrant selection and second-generation educational adaptation. This study provides a first step towards understanding the implications of immigrant selection, and challenges arguments that certain national-origin groups value education more than others by highlighting how the inherently unequal structure of the immigration process itself produces immigrant groups with varying levels of relative pre-migration educational attainment. Thus, the persistent puzzle of why some national-origin groups excel in school while others lag behind is illuminated by understanding how inequalities in the relative pre-migration educational attainments of immigrants are often reproduced among their children in the United States.

Appendix

Table A3.1. Data Collected on Immigrants and Home Country Populations

Country of Origin	Year of Country Data	Average Year of Migration	IPUMS Data Year	Years of Migration of Immigrants Selected	Ages of Immigrants Selected*
Italy	1961	1960-64	1970, 1960	1955-65	25+ in 1961
Canada	1961	1965-69	1970	1960-70	25+ in 1961
Hungary	1963	1960-64	1970	1955-70	25+ in 1963
Ireland	1966	1965-74	1970, 1980	1960-74	25+ in 1966
Iran	1966	1980-81	1980, 1990	1970-90	25+ in 1966
Puerto Rico	1970	1965-69	1970	1965-69	25+ in 1970
Poland	1970	1970-74	1970, 1980	1965-79	20+ in 1970
Russia	1970	1970-74	1980, 1990	1970-84	25+ in 1970
Japan	1970	1975-79	1980, 1990	1970-84	25+ in 1970
Dom. Rep.	1970	1980-81	1980, 1990	1975-86	20+ in 1970
Greece	1971	1965-69	1970, 1980	1960-74	25+ in 1971
Yugoslavia	1971	1965-69	1970, 1980	1960-75	18+ in 1971
Netherlands	1971	1965-69	1970, 1980	1960-75	18+ in 1971
Nicaragua	1971	1982-84	1980, 1990	1975-90	20+ in 1971
Columbia	1973	1980-81	1980, 1990	1970-86	20+ in 1973
Mexico	1980	1980-81	1980, 1990	1975-84	20+ in 1980
Philippines	1980	1980-81	1980, 1990	1975-84	20+ in 1980
Thailand	1980	1980-81	1980, 1990	1975-90	20+ in 1980
Korea	1980	1982-84	1980, 1990	1975-86	20+ in 1980
Cuba	1981	1965-74	1970, 1980	1965-74	25-49 in 1981
Portugal	1981	1975-79	1980, 1990	1970-84	20+ in 1981
Hong Kong	1981	1980-81	1980, 1990	1975-86	20+ in 1981
India	1981	1982-84	1980, 1990	1975-86	20+ in 1982
Guatemala	1981	1982-84	1980, 1990	1975-90	20+ in 1982
Peru	1981	1982-84	1980, 1990	1975-90	20+ in 1981
China	1982	1980-81	1980, 1990	1975-86	20+ in 1982
Ecuador	1982	1980-81	1980, 1990	1975-90	18+ in 1980
Jamaica	1982	1980-81	1980, 1990	1975-86	25+ in 1989
Haiti	1982	1980-81	1980, 1990	1975-86	20+ in 1982
Honduras	1983	1980-81	1980, 1990	1975-90	18+ in 1980
Vietnam	1989	1982-84	1980, 1990	1975-86	25+ in 1989
El Salvador	1992	1982-84	1990	1980-90	25+ in 1992

Note: The data source for all countries of origin except Puerto Rico is
UNESCO; the data source for Puerto Rico is the Census.

* *All immigrants selected were at least 22 years old when they migrated to the U.S.*

Table A4.1. National-Origin Groups' Selectivity and Socioeconomic Status by Dependent Variables

Country of Origin	Group Selectivity (NDI)	Group SES	Expectations	Aspirations	Parents' Aspirations	N
Mexico	0.208	0.000	0.640	0.487	0.515	594
El Salvador	0.350	0.054	0.800	0.680	0.640	25
Cuba	0.399	0.227	0.884	0.722	0.677	959
Honduras	0.454	0.089	0.833	0.571	0.571	42
Dominican Republic	0.490	0.172	0.711	0.474	0.553	76
Ecuador	0.496	0.281	0.889	0.704	0.481	27
Korea	0.525	0.571	0.800	0.667	0.667	15
Guatemala	0.551	0.058	0.64	0.440	0.520	25
Vietnam	0.595	0.422	0.861	0.699	0.672	302
Philippines	0.597	0.656	0.862	0.717	0.645	718
Hong Kong	0.612	0.763	1.000	0.765	0.706	17
Colombia	0.625	0.393	0.867	0.691	0.790	181
Peru	0.645	0.421	0.964	0.821	0.821	28
Jamaica	0.648	0.566	0.847	0.754	0.729	118
Japan	0.670	0.772	0.920	0.720	0.640	25
Nicaragua	0.670	0.276	0.868	0.771	0.779	280
China	0.671	0.374	0.943	0.800	0.714	35
Haiti	0.720	0.188	0.811	0.674	0.667	132
India	0.859	1.000	0.944	0.944	0.889	18

References

Abbott, Edith. 1969. *Historical Aspects of the Immigration Problem: Select Documents*. New York: Arno Press.

Ainsworth-Darnell, James W. and Douglas B. Downey. 1998. "Assessing the Oppositional Culture Explanation for Racial/Ethnic Differences in School Performance." *American Sociological Review* 63:536-553.

Alba, Richard D. and Victor Nee. 1997. "Rethinking Assimilation Theory for a New Era of Immigration." *International Migration Review* 31:826-874.

— 2003. *Remaking the American Mainstream: Assimilation and Contemporary Immigration*. Cambridge, MA and London (U.K.): Harvard University Press.

Alexander, Karl L. and Martha A. Cook. 1979. "The Motivational Relevance of Educational Plans: Questioning the Conventional Wisdom." *Social Psychology Quarterly* 42:202-213.

Alexander, Karl L., Doris R. Entwisle, and Samuel D. Bedinger. 1994. "When Expectations Work: Race and Socioeconomic Differences in School Performance." *Social Psychology Quarterly* 57:283-299.

Banks, James A. 1988. "Ethnicity, Class, Cognitive, and Motivational Styles: Research and Teaching Implications." *Journal of Negro Education* 57:452-66.

Bankston, Carl L. and Min Zhou. 2002. "Social Capital and Immigrant Children's Achievement." in *Schooling and Social Capital in Diverse Cultures*, 13:13-39, edited by B. Fuller and E. Hannum.

Bean, Frank, Harley Browning, and W. Parker Frisbie. 1985. "What the 1980 Census Tells Us About the Character of Illegal and Legal Mexican Immigrants." Population Research Center, UT Austin.

Bean, Frank D., Jorge Chapa, Ruth R. Berg, and Kathryn A. Sowards. 1994. "Educational and Sociodemographic Incorporation among Hispanic Immigrants to the United States." Pp. 73-99 in *Immigration and Ethnicity: the Integration of America's Newest Arrivals*, edited by B. Edmonston and J. S. Passel. Washington, D.C. Lanham, MD: Urban Institute Press; Distributed by University Press of America.

Bean, Frank D. and Gillian Stevens. 2003. *America's Newcomers and the Dynamics of Diversity*. New York: Russell Sage Foundation.

Blau, Peter Michael and Otis Dudley Duncan. 1967. *The American Occupational Structure*. New York: Wiley.

Bonacich, Edna. 1976. "Advanced Capitalism and Black/White Race Relations in the United States: A Split Labor Market Interpretation." *American Sociological Review* 41:34-51.

Borjas, George J. 1987. "Self-Selection and the Earnings of Immigrants." *The American Economic Review* 77:531-553.

—. 1990a. *Friends or Strangers: The Impact of Immigrants on the U.S. Economy*. New York: Basic Books, Inc.

.— 1990. "Self-Selection and the Earnings of Immigrants - reply." *American Economic Review* 80:305-308.

—. 1991. "Immigration and Self-Selection." in *Immigration, Trade, and the Labor Market*, edited by J. M. Abowd. Chicago: The University of Chicago Press.

— 1992a. "Ethnic Capital and Intergenerational Mobility." *Quarterly Journal of Economics*, Feb, pp. 123-150.

—. 1992b. "National Origin and the Skills of Immigrants in the Postwar Period." Pp. 17-47 in *Immigration and the Workforce: Economic Consequences for the United States and Source Areas*, edited by G. Borjas and R. B. Freeman. Chicago: University of Chicago Press.

—. 1993. "The Intergenerational Mobility of Immigrants." *Journal of Labor Economics* 11:113-135.

—. 1994. "Long-Run Convergence of Ethnic Skill Differentials - the Children and Grandchildren of the Great Migration." *Industrial & Labor Relations Review* 47:553-573.

—. 1996. "The Earnings of Mexican Immigrants in the United States." *Journal of Development Economics* 51:69-98.

—. 1999. *Heaven's Door: Immigration Policy and the American Economy*. Princeton, NJ: Princeton University Press.

—. 2001. "Long-Run Convergence of Ethnic Skill Differentials, Revisited." *Demography* 38:357-361.

—. 2004. "Economic Assimilation: Trouble Ahead." Pp. 199-220 in *Reinventing the Melting Pot: The New Immigrants and What It Means To Be American*, edited by T. Jacoby. New York: Basic Books.

Bourdieu, Pierre. 1973. "Cultural Reproduction and Social Reproduction." Pp. 71-112 in *Knowledge, Education, and Cultural Change*, edited by R. Brown. London: Tavistock.

Bourdieu, Pierre and Jean Claude Passeron. 1977. *Reproduction in Education, Society and Culture*. London; Beverly Hills: Sage Publications.

Bowles, Samuel and Herbert Gintis. 1976. *Schooling in Capitalist America: Educational Reform and the Contradictions of Economic Life*. New York: Basic Books.

Bray, David. 1984. "Economic Development: The Middle Class and
    International Migration in the Dominican Republic." *International
    Migration Review* 18:217-236.

Briggs, Vernon M. 1975. "The Need for a More Restrictive Border Policy."
    Social Science Quarterly 56:477-484.

California Postsecondary Education Commission. 2005. "Are They Going?
    University Enrollment and Eligibility for African Americans and
    Latinos." Fact-sheet 5-03.

Campbell, Richard T. 1983. "Status Attainment Research: End of the
    Beginning or Beginning of the End." *Sociology of Education* 56:47-
    62.

Caplan, Nathan, Marcella H. Choy, and John K. Whitmore. 1992. *Children of
    the Boat People: A Study of Educational Success.* Ann Arbor:
    University of Michigan Press.

Carliner, Geoffrey. 1980. "Wages, Earnings, and Hours of 1st, 2nd, and 3rd
    Generation American Males." *Economic Inquiry* 18:87-102.

Caudill, William and George DeVos. 1956. "Achievement, Culture and
    Personality: The Case of the Japanese Americans." *American
    Anthropologist* 58:1102-1126.

Chapa, Jorge. 1990. "The Myth of Hispanic Progress." *Journal of Hispanic
    Policy* 4:3-18.

Chavez, Linda. 1991. *Out of the Barrio: Toward A New Politics of Hispanic
    Assimilation*: HarperCollins.

Cheng, Lucie and Philip Q. Yang. 1996. "Asians: The 'Model Minority'
    Deconstructed." Pp. 305-344 in *Ethnic Los Angeles*, edited by R.
    Waldinger and M. Bozorgmehr. New York: Russell Sage Foundation.

Cheng, Simon and Brian Starks. 2002. "Racial Differences in the Effects of
    Significant Others on Students' Educational Expectations." *Sociology
    of Education* 75:306-327.

Chiswick, Barry R. 1978. "The Effect of Americanization on the Earnings of Foreign-born Men." *Journal of Political Economy* 86:897-921.

——. 1986. "Is the New Immigration Less Skilled than the Old?" *Journal of Labor Economics* 4:168-92.

——. 2000. "Are Immigrants Favorably Self-Selected?" Pp. 61-76 in *Migration Theory: Talking across Disciplines*, edited by C. B. Brettell and J. F. Hollifield. New York: Routledge.

Cobb-Clark, Deborah A. 1993. "Immigrant Selectivity and Wages - the Evidence for Women." *American Economic Review* 83:986-993.

Coleman, James S. 1988. "Social Capital in the Creation of Human Capital." *American Journal of Sociology* 94:S95-S120.

Coleman, James S., Ernest Q. Campbell, Carol J. Hobson, James McPartland, Alexander Mood, Frederic D. Weinfeld, and Robert L. York. 1966. *Equality of Educational Opportunity*. Washington D.C.: U.S. Government Printing Office.

CILS, Children of Immigrants Longitudinal Study. 2005. Alejandro Portes and Rubén Rumbaut. New Jersey: Center for Migration and Development, Princeton University (http://cmd.princeton.edu/cils.shtml) (distributor).

Covello, Leonard and Francesco Cordasco. 1967. *The Social Background of the Italo-American School Child. A Study of the Southern Italian Family Mores and Their Effect on the School Situation in Italy and America.* Leiden: E. J. Brill.

Davies, Mark and Denise B. Kandel. 1981. "Parental and Peer Influences on Adolescents' Educational Plans: Some Further Evidence." *American Journal of Sociology* 87:363-387.

Deininger, Klaus and Squire, Lyn. "Deininger and Squire Data Set: A New Data Set Measuring Income Inequality." *The World Bank Group. Economic Growth Research.* http://www.worldbank.org/research/growth/dddeisqu.htm

Donato, Katharine M. 1993. "Current Trends and Patterns of Female Migration: Evidence from Mexico." *International Migration Review* 27:748-771

Driscoll, Anne K. 1999. "Risk of High School Dropout among Immigrant and Native Hispanic Youth." *International Migration Review* 33:857-875.

Duncan, Otis Dudley, David L. Featherman, and Beverly Duncan. 1972. *Socioeconomic Background and Achievement*. New York: Seminar Press.

Durand, Jorge, Douglas S. Massey, and Rene M. Zenteno 2001. "Mexican Immigration to the United States: Continuities and Changes." *Latin American Research Review*, Winter, pp. 107.

Entwisle, Doris R. and Leslie A. Hayduk. 1978. *Too Great Expectations: The Academic Outlook of Young Children*. Baltimore: John Hopkins University Press.

Espiritu,Yen Le. 2003. "We Don't Sleep Around Like White Girls Do": Family, Culture and Gender in Filipina American Lives." Pp. 263-286 in *Gender and U.S. Immigration: Contemporary Trends*, edited by P. Hondagneu-Sotelo. Berkeley, CA: University of California Press.

Farley, Reynolds and Richard Alba. 2002. "The New Second Generation in the United States." *International Migration Review* 36:669-701.

Feliciano, Cynthia. 2001. "The Benefits of Biculturalism: Exposure to Immigrant Culture and Dropping out of School among Asian and Latino Youths." *Social Science Quarterly* 82:866-880.

Fernandez, Roberto M. and Francois Nielsen. 1986. "Bilingualism and Hispanic Scholastic Achievement: Some Baseline Results." *Social Science Research* 14:43-70.

Foner, Nancy. 2000. *From Ellis Island to JFK: New York's Two Great Waves of Immigration*. New Haven, New York: Yale University Press, Russell Sage Foundation.

Fussell, Elizabeth. 2004. "Sources of Mexico's Migration Stream: Rural, Urban, and Border Migrants to the United States." *Social Forces* 82:937-967.

Fussell, Elizabeth and Douglas S. Massey . 2004. "The Limits to Cumulative Causation: International Migration from Mexican Urban Areas." *Demography* 41:151-171.

Gans, Herbert J. 1982. *The Urban Villagers:Group and Class in the Life of Italian-Americans*. New York, London: Free Press, Collier Macmillan Publishers.

—. 1992. "Second Generation Decline: Scenarios for the Economic and Ethnic Futures of the Post-1965 American Immigrants." *Ethnic and Racial Studies* 15:251-270.

—. 2000. "Filling in Some Holes: Six Areas of Needed Immigration Research."Pp.76-89 in *Immigration Research for a New Century*, edited by N. Foner, R. G. Rumbaut, and S. J. Gold. New York: Russell Sage Foundation.

Garrison, Howard H. 1982. "Trends in Educational and Occupational Aspirations of High-School Males - Black-White Comparisons." *Sociology of Education* 55:53-63.

Gibson, Margaret A. 1988. *Accommodation without Assimilation: Sikh Immigrants in an American High School*. Ithaca: Cornell University Press.

Glaser, William A. 1978. *The Brain Drain: Emigration and Return*. Oxford: Pergamon Press.

Glazer, Nathan and Daniel P. Moynihan. 1963. *Beyond the Melting Pot; the Negroes, Puerto Ricans, Jews, Italians, and Irish of New York City*. Cambridge, MA: M.I.T. Press.

Glick, Jennifer E. and Michael J. White. 2004. "Post-Secondary School Participation of Immigrant and Native Youth: The Role of Familial Resources and Educational Expectations." *Social Science Research* 33:272-299.

Goldenberg, Claude, Ronald Gallimore, Leslie Reese, and Helen Garnier. 2001. "Cause or Effect? A Longitudinal Study of Immigrant Latino Parents' Aspirations and Expectations, and their Children's School Performance." *American Educational Research Journal* 38:547-582.

Goldscheider, Calvin and Alan S. Zuckerman. 1984. *The Transformation of the Jews.* Chicago: University of Chicago Press.

Gonzalez, Gabriella Christina. 2002. "Family Background, Ethnicity, and Immigration Status: Predicting School Success for Asian and Latino Students." Sociology Dissertation, Harvard University, Cambridge.

Gordon, Milton Myron. 1964. *Assimilation in American Life: The Role of Race, Religion, and National Origins.* New York: Oxford University Press.

Goyette, Kimberly A. and Gilberto Q. Conchas. 2002. "Family and Non-family Roots of Social Capital among Vietnamese and Mexican-American Children." in *Schooling and Social Capital in Diverse Cultures*, edited by B. Fuller and E. Hannum. Oxford: Elsevier Science Ltd.

Goyette, Kimberly and Yu Xie. 1999. "Educational Expectations of Asian American Youths: Determinants and Ethnic Differences." *Sociology of Education* 72:22-36.

Green, David A. 1999. "Immigrant Occupational Attainment: Assimilation and Mobility over Time." *Journal of Labor Economics* 17:49-79.

Grogger, Jeffrey and Stephen J. Trejo. 2002. "Falling Behind or Moving Up? The Intergenerational Progress of Mexican Americans." Public Policy Institute of California, San Francisco, CA.

Grubel, Herbert G. and Anthony Scott. 1977. *The Brain Drain: Determinants, Measurement and Welfare Effects.* Waterloo, Ontario: Wilfrid Laurier University Press.

Haller, Archibald O. and Alejandro Portes. 1973. "Status Attainment Processes." *Sociology of Education* 46:51-91.

Hanson, Sandra L. 1994. "Lost Talent: Unrealized Educational Aspirations and Expectations among U.S. Youths." *Sociology of Education* 67:159-183.

Hao, Lingxin and Melissa Bonstead-Bruns 1998. "Parent-Child Differences in Educational Expectations and the Academic Achievement of Immigrant and Native Students." *Sociology of Education*, 71:175-198.

Hauser, Robert M. and Douglas K. Anderson. 1991. "Post-high School Plans and Aspirations of Black and White High School Seniors: 1976-86." *Sociology of Education* 64:263-277.

Hauser, Robert M. and David L. Featherman. 1977. *The Process of Stratification: Trends and Analyses*. New York: Academic Press.

Hedges, Larry V. and Amy Nowell. 1998. "Black-White Test Score Convergence since 1965." in Pp.149-181 *The Black-White Test Score Gap*, edited by C. Jencks and M. Phillips. Washington D.C.: Brookings Institution Press.

Herrnstein, Richard J. and Charles A. Murray. 1994. *The Bell Curve: Intelligence and Class Structure in American Life*. New York: Free Press.

Hirschman, Charles. 2001. "The Educational Enrollment of Immigrant Youth: A test of the Segmented-Assimilation Hypothesis." *Demography* 38:317-336.

Hirschman, Charles and Luis M. Falcon. 1985. "The Educational Attainment of Religio-Ethnic Groups in the United States." *Research in Sociology of Education and Socialization* 5:83-120.

Hirschman, Charles and Morrison G. Wong. 1986. "The Extraordinary Educational Attainment of Asian-Americans: A Search for Historical Evidence and Explanations." *Social Forces* 65:1-27.

IPUMS, Integrated Public Use Microdata Series: Version 2.0. 1997. Steven Ruggles and Matthew Sobek. Minneapolis: Historical Census

Projects, University of Minnesota (http://www.ipums.umn.edu)
(distributor). Washington, D.C.: U.S. Department of Commerce,
Bureau of the Census (producer).

Jasso, Guillermina and Mark R. Rosenzweig. 1986. "What's In a Name?
Country-of-origin Influences on the Earnings of Immigrants in the
United States." *Research in Human Capital and Development* 4:75-
106.

Jencks, Christopher, James Crouse, and Peter Mueser. 1983. "The Wisconsin
Model of Status Attainment - A National Replication with Improved
Measures of Ability and Aspiration." *Sociology of Education* 56:3-
19.

Jencks, Christopher and Meredith Phillips. 1998. *The Black-White Test Score
Gap*. Washington, D.C.: Brookings Institution Press.

Jencks, Christopher, Marshall Smith, Henry Acland, Mary Jo Bane, David
Cohen, Herbert Gintis, Barbara Heyns, and Stephan Michelson. 1972.
*Inequality: A Reassessment of the Effect of Family and Schooling in
America*. New York: Harper & Row.

Kao, Grace. 2000. "Group Images and Possible Selves among Adolescents:
Linking Stereotypes to Expectations by Race and Ethnicity."
Sociological Forum 15:407-430.

—. 2002. "Ethnic Differences in Parents' Educational Aspirations.".in
Schooling and Social Capital in Diverse Cultures, 13: 85-103 edited
by B. Fuller and E. Hannum.

—. 2004. "Parental Influences on the Educational Outcomes of Immigrant
Youth." *International Migration Review* 38:427-449.

Kao, Grace and Marta Tienda. 1995. "Optimism and Achievement: The
Educational Performance of Immigrant Youth." *Social Science
Quarterly* 76:1-19.

—. 1998. "Educational Aspirations of Minority Youth." *American Journal of
Education* 106:349-384.

Kasinitz, Philip, John Mollenkopf, and Mary C. Waters. 2002. "Becoming American/Becoming New Yorkers: Immigrant Incorporation in a Majority Minority City." *International Migration Review* 36:1020-1036.

Kerckhoff, Alan C. and Richard T. Campbell. 1977. "Black-White Differences in the Educational Attainment Process." *Sociology of Education* 50:15-27.

Lamm, Richard D. and Gary Imhoff. 1985. *The Immigration Time Bomb:The Fragmenting of America*. New York: Truman Talley Books.

Landale, Nancy S. 1994. "Migration and the Latino Family - The Union Formation Behavior of Puerto-Rican Women." *Demography* 31:133-157.

Landale, Nancy S. R. S. Oropesa, and Bridget K. Gorman. 2000. "Migration and Infant Death: Assimilation or Selective Migration among Puerto Ricans?" *American Sociological Review* 65:888-909.

Lee, Everett S. 1966. "A Theory of Migration." *Demography* 3:47-57.

Lieberson, Stanley. 1976. "Rank-Sum Comparisons between Groups." *Sociological Methodology* 7:276-291.

—. 1980. *A Piece of the Pie: Blacks and White Immigrants since 1880*. Berkeley: University of California Press.

Livingston, Gretchen and Joan R. Kahn. 2002. "An American Dream Unfulfilled: The Limited Mobility of Mexican Americans." *Social Science Quarterly* 83:1003-1012.

Lobo, Arun Peter and Joseph J. Salvo. 1998a. "Changing U.S. Immigration Law and the Occupational Selectivity of Asian Immigrants." *International Migration Review* 32:737-760

—. 1998b. "Resurgent Irish Immigration to the US in the 1980s and Early 1990s - a Socio-Demographic Profile." *International Migration Review* 36:257-280.

Long, Larry H. 1973. "Migration Differentials by Education and Occupation - Trends and Variations." *Demography* 10:243-258.

Macleod,Jay.1995.Ain't No *Makin' It: Aspirations and Attainment in a Low-Income Neighborhood.* Boulder: Westview Press.

Marcelli, Enrico A. and Wayne A. Cornelius. 2001. "The Changing Profile of Mexican Migrants to the United States: New Evidence from California and Mexico." *Latin American Research Review* 36:105-131.

Mare, Robert D. 1995. "Changes in Educational Attainment and School Enrollment." in Pp.155-213*State of the Union: America in the 1990s,* edited by R. Farley. New York: Russell Sage Foundation.

Massey, Douglas and Felipe Garcia Espana. 1987. "The Social Process of International Migration." *Science* 237:733-738.

Massey, Douglas S. 1986. "The Settlement Process among Mexican Migrants to the United States." *American Sociological Review* 51:670-684.

—. 1987a. "Do Undocumented Immigrants Earn Lower Wages than Legal Immigrants?" *International Migration Review* 21:236-274.

—. 1987b. "Understanding Mexican Migration to the United States." *American Journal of Sociology* 92:1372-1403.

—. 1988. "Economic Development and International Migration in Comparative Perspective." *Population and Development Review* 14:383-413.

—. 1999. "Why Does Immigration Occur? A Theoretical Synthesis." Pp. 34-52 in *Handbook of International Migration,* edited by C. Hirschman, P. Kasinitz, and J. DeWind. New York: Russell Sage Foundation.

Massey, Douglas S., Rafael Alarcón, Jorge Durand, and Humberto Gonzalez. 1987. *Return to Aztlan: The Social Process of International Migration from Western Mexico.* Berkeley: University of California Press.

Massey, Douglas S., Joaquin Arango, Graeme Hugo, Ali Kouaouci, Adela
    Pellegrino, and J. Edward Taylor. 1993. "Theories of International
    Migration - A Review and Appraisal." *Population and Development
    Review* 19:431-466.

Massey, Douglas S. and Nancy A. Denton. 1993. *American Apartheid:
    Segregation and the Making of the Underclass*. Cambridge, MA:
    Harvard University Press.

Massey, Douglas S. and Kristen E. Espinosa. 1997. "What's Driving Mexico-
    U.S. Migration? A Theoretical, Empirical, and Policy Analysis."
    American Journal of Sociolgy 102:939-999.

Matute-Bianchi, Maria Eugenia. 1991. "Situational Ethnicity and Patterns of
    School Performance among Immigrant and Nonimmigrant Mexican-
    Descent Students.".Pp.205-247 in *Minority Status and Schooling: A
    Comparative Study of Immigrant and Involuntary Minorities*, edited
    by M. Gibson and J. Ogbu. New York: Garland Publishing.

McCarthy, Kevin and R.B. Valdez. 1985. *Current and Future Effects of
    Mexican Immigration in California*. R-3365-CR. Santa Monica, CA:
    The Rand Corporation.

Melendez, Edwin. 1994. "Puerto-Rican Migration and Occupational
    Selectivity, 1982-1981." *International Migration Review* 28:49-67.

Menjívar, Cecilia. 1993. "History, Economy and Politics: Macro and Micro-
    Level Factors in Recent Salvadorean Migration to the U.S." *Journal
    of Refugee Studies* 6:350-371.

Ogbu, John U. 1974. *The Next Generation; an Ethnography of Education in an
    Urban Neighborhood*. New York: Academic Press.

—. 1991. *Cultural Models and Educational Strategies of Non-dominant
    Peoples*. New York, NY: City College Workshop Center.

—. 1991. "Immigrant and Involuntary Minorities in Comparative Perspective."
    Pp. 3-33 in *Minority Status and Schooling: A Comparative Study of*

Immigrant and Involuntary Minorities, edited by M. A. Gibson and J. U. Ogbu. New York: Garland Publishing.

—. 2003. *Black American Students in an Affluent Suburb: A Study of Academic Disengagement*. Mahwah, N.J.: L. Erlbaum Associates.

Ortiz, Vilma. 1986. "Changes in the Characteristics of Puerto Rican Migrants from 1955 to 1980." *International Migration Review* 20:612-628.

Palloni, Alberto, Douglas. S. Massey, Miguel Ceballos, Kristin Espinosa, and Michael Spittel. 2001. "Social Capital and International Migration: A Test using Information on Family Networks." *American Journal of Sociology* 106:1262-1298.

Park, Robert. 1928. "Human Migration and the Marginal Man." *American Journal of Sociology* 33:881-893.

Perlmann, Joel. 1988. *Ethnic Differences: Schooling and Social Structure among the Irish, Italians, Jews, and Blacks in an American City, 1880-1935*. Cambridge; New York: Cambridge University Press.

—. 2001. "Young Mexican Americans, Blacks, and Whites in Recent Years: Schooling and Teen Motherhood as Indicators of Strengths and Risks." The Jerome Levy Institute of Bard College.

Perlmann, Joel and Roger Waldinger. 1997. "Second Generation Decline? Children of Immigrants, Past and Present a Reconsideration." *International Migration Review* 31:893-922.

Porter, James N. 1974. "Race, Socialization and Mobility in Educational and Early Occupational Attainment." *American Sociological Review* 39:303-16.

Portes, Alejandro. 1979. "Illegal Immigrants and the International System: Lessons from Recent Legal Mexican Immigrants to the United States." *Social Problems* 26:425-438.

—. 2003. "Ethnicities: Children of Migrants in America." *Development* 46:42-52.

Portes, Alejandro and Jozsef Borocz 1989. "Contemporary Immigration - Theoretical Perspectives on its Determinants and Modes of Incorporation." *International Migration Review* 23:606-630.

Portes, Alejandro and Dag Macleod. 1996. "Educational Progress of Children of Immigrants - the Roles of Class, Ethnicity, and School Context." *Sociology of Education* 69:255-275.

Portes, Alejandro and Rubén G. Rumbaut. 1996. *Immigrant America:A Portrait.* Berkeley: University of California Press.

—. 2001. *Legacies:The Story of the Immigrant Second Generation.* Berkeley New York: University of California Press.

Portes, Alejandro and Kenneth L Wilson. 1976. "Black-White Differences in Educational Attainment." *American Sociological Review* 41:414-431.

Portes, Alejandro and Min Zhou. 1993. "The New Second Generation - Segmented Assimilation and Its Variants." *The Annals of the American Academy of Political and Social Science* 530:74-96.

Qian, Zhenchao and Sampson Lee Blair. 1999. "Racial/Ethnic Differences in Educational Aspirations of High School Seniors." *Sociological Perspectives* 42:605-617.

Ramos, Fernando. 1992. "Out-Migration and Return Migration of Puerto Ricans." Pp. 49-66 in *Immigration and the Work Force: Economic Consequences for the United States and Source Areas*, edited by G. J. Borjas and R. B. Freeman. Chicago: University of Chicago Press.

Ravenstein, E.G. 1885. "The Laws of Migration." *Journal of the Royal Statistical Society* 48:167-227.

Reimers, David M. 2005. *Other Immigrants: The Global Origins of the American People.* New York: New York University Press.

Roberts, Bryan R., Reanne Frank, and Fernando Lozano-Ascencio. 1999. "Transnational Migrant Communities and Mexican Migration to the US." *Ethnic & Racial Studies* 22:238-266.

Roy, Andrew D. 1951. "Some Thoughts on the Distribution of Earnings." *Oxford Economic Papers* 3:135-46.

Rumbaut, Rubén G. 1995. "The New Californians: Comparative Research Findings on the Educational Progress of Immigrant Children." in Pp.17-69*California's Immigrant Children: Theory Research, and Implications for Educational Policy*, edited by R. G. Rumbaut and W. A. Cornelius. San Diego: Center for U.S.-Mexican Studies, U.C. San Diego.

—. 1996. "Origins and Destinies: Immigration, Race, and Ethnicity in Contemporary America." in Pp. 21-42.*Origins and Destinies: Immigration, Race, and Ethnicity in America*, edited by S. Pedraza and R. G. Rumbaut. Belmont, CA: Wadsworth Publishing.

—. 1997. "Ties that Bind: Immigration and Immigrant Families in the United States." Pp. 3-46 in *Immigration and the Family: Research and Policy on U.S. Immigrants*, edited by A. Booth, A. C. Crouter, and N. Landale. Mahwah, N.J.: Lawrence Erlbaum Associates.

—. 1999. "Assimilation and Its Discontents: Ironies and Paradoxes." Pp. 172-195 in *The Handbook of International Migration: The American Experience*, edited by C. Hirschman, P. Kasinitz, and J. DeWind. New York: Russell Sage Foundation.

Rumbaut, Rubén G. and Alejandro Portes. 2001. *Ethnicities: Children of Immigrants in America*. Berkeley, New York: University of California Press.

Schneider, Barbara and Yongsook Lee. 1990. "A Model for Academic Success: The School and Home Environment of East Asian Students." *Anthropology and Education Quarterly* 21:358-377.

Schultz, T. Paul. 1984. "The Schooling and Health of Children of U.S. Immigrants and Natives." *Research in Population Economics* 5:251-288.

Sewell, William H., Archibald O Haller, and George W. Ohlendorf. 1970. "The Educational and Early Occupational Status Attainment Process:

Replication and Revision." *American Sociological Review* 35:1014-1027.

Sewell, William H., Archibald O. Haller, and Alejandro Portes. 1969. "The Educational and Early Occupational Attainment Process." *American Sociological Review* 34:82-92.

Sewell, William H. and Robert M. Hauser. 1975. *Education, Occupation, and Earnings*. New York: Academic Press.

—. 1980. "The Wisconsin Longitudinal Study of Social and Psychological Factors in Aspirations and Achievements." *Research in Sociology of Education and Socialization* 1:59-99.

Sewell, William H. and Vimal P. Shah. 1968a. "Parents' Education and Children's Educational Aspirations and Achievements." *American Sociological Review* 33:191-209.

—. 1968b. "Social Class, Parental Encouragement, and Educational Aspirations." *The American Journal of Sociology* 73:559-572.

Shryock, Henry S. and Charles B. Nam. 1965. "Educational Selectivity of Interregional Migration." *Social Forces* 43:299-310.

Smith, James P. 2003. "Assimilation across the Latino Generations." *American Economic Review* 93:315-319.

Sowell, Thomas. 1981. *Ethnic America:A History*. New York: Basic Books.

St-Hilaire, Aonghas. 2002. "The Social Adaptation of Children of Mexican Immigrants: Educational Aspirations Beyond Junior High School." *Social Science Quarterly* 83:1026-1043.

Stanton-Salazar, Ricardo D. and Sanford M. Dornbusch. 1995. "Social Capital and the Reproduction of Inequality - Information Networks among Mexican-Origin High School Students." *Sociology of Education* 68:116-135.

Stark, Oded and David E. Bloom. 1985. "The New Economics of Labor Migration." *The American Economic Review, Papers and Proceedings of the Ninety-Seventh Annual Meeting of the American Economic Association* 75:173-178.

Steinberg, Laurence. 1996. "Ethnicity and Educational Achievement." *American Educator* Summer.

Steinberg, Laurence D., B. Bradford Brown, and Sanford M. Dornbusch. 1996. *Beyond the Classroom: Why School Reform has Failed and What Parents Need to do.* New York: Simon & Schuster.

Steinberg, Stephen. 1981. *The Ethnic Myth: Race, Ethnicity, and Class in America.* New York: Atheneum.

Suárez-Orozco, Carola and Marcelo M. Suárez-Orozco. 2001. *Children of Immigration.* Cambridge, Mass.: Harvard University Press.

—. 1995. "The Cultural Patterning of Achievement Motivation: A Comparison of Mexican, Mexican Immigrant, Mexican American, and Non-Latino White American Students." in Pp.161-190. *California's Immigrant Children: Theory Research, and Implications for Educational Policy,* edited by R. G. Rumbaut and W. Cornelius. San Diego: Center for U.S.-Mexican Studies, U.C. San Diego.

Sue, Stanley and Sumie Okazaki 1990. "Asian-American Educational Achievements: A Phenomenon in Search of an Explanation." *American Psychologist*, August: pp. 913.

Suval, Elizabeth M. and C. Horace Hamilton. 1965. "Some New Evidence on Educational Selectivity in Migration to and from the South." *Social Forces* 43:536-547.

Taylor, J. Edward. 1986. "Differential Migration, Networks, Information, and Risk." Pp. 141-71 in *Research in Human Capital and Development,* edited by O. Stark. Greenwich, Conn: Jai Press.

—. 1987. "Undocumented Mexico-U.S. Migration and the Return to Households in Rural Mexico." *American Journal of Agricultural Economics* 69:626-638.

Teitelbaum, Michael. 1980. "Right versus Right: Immigration and Refugee Policy in the United States." *Foreign Affairs* 59:21-59.

Thernstrom, Stephan. 1973. *The Other Bostonians;Poverty and Progress in the American Metropolis, 1880-1970.* Cambridge, Mass.: Harvard University Press.

Tolnay, Stewart E. 1998. "Educational Selection in the Migration of Southern Blacks, 1880-1990." *Social Forces* 77:487-514.

Treiman, Donald J. and Hye-kyung Lee. 1996. "Income Differences among 31 Ethnic Groups in Los Angeles." in Pp.37-82*Social Differentiation and Social Inequality: Essays in Honor of John Pock*, edited by J. N. Baron, D. B. Grusky, and D. J. Treiman. Boulder, CO: Westview Press.

Treiman, Donald J., Vivian Lew, Hye-Kyung Lee, and Thad A. Brown. 1986. "Occupational Status Attainment among Ethnic Groups in Los Angeles."Working Paper, Institute for Social Science Research 2(1).

UNESCO. 1975. United Nations Educational, Scientific and Cultural Organization Statistical Yearbook. UNESCO Publishing and Berman Press.

UNESCO. 1978-79. United Nations Educational, Scientific and Cultural Organization Statistical Yearbook. UNESCO Publishing and Berman Press.

UNESCO. 1989. United Nations Educational, Scientific and Cultural Organization Statistical Yearbook. UNESCO Publishing and Berman Press.

UNESCO. 1992. United Nations Educational, Scientific and Cultural Organization Statistical Yearbook. UNESCO Publishing and Berman Press.

UNESCO. 1993. United Nations Educational, Scientific and Cultural Organization Statistical Yearbook. UNESCO Publishing and Berman Press.

UNESCO. 1995. United Nations Educational, Scientific and Cultural Organization Statistical Yearbook. UNESCO Publishing and Berman Press.

UNESCO. 1997. United Nations Educational, Scientific and Cultural Organization Statistical Yearbook. UNESCO Publishing and Berman Press.

UNESCO, United Nations Educational, Scientific and Cultural Organization. 2001. (http://www.unesco.org/).

Vas-Zoltan, Peter. 1976. *The Brain Drain: An Anomaly of International Relations*. Budapest: A.W. Sijthoff, Leyden.

Vernez, Georges. 1997. "Education's Hispanic Challenge." in Pp.1-24 *Educational and Economic Prospects of the Second Generation*. Levy Economics Institute.

Vernez, Georges and Allan Abrahamse. 1996. "How Immigrants Fare in U.S. Education." Institute on Education and Training; Center for Research on Immigration Policy, Santa Monica, CA.

Waldinger, Roger. 1996. *Still the Promised City? African-Americans and New Immigrants in Postindustrial New York*. Cambridge, Mass.: Harvard University Press.

Waldinger, Roger and Cynthia Feliciano. 2004. "Will the New Second Generation Experience 'Downward Assimilation'? Segmented Assimilation Re-assessed." *Ethnic and Racial Studies* 27:376-402.

Waldinger, Roger and Michael Lichter. 1996. "Anglos: Beyond Ethnicity?" Pp. 413-441 in *Ethnic Los Angeles*, edited by R. Waldinger and M. Bozorgmehr. New York: Russell Sage Foundation.

Waters, Mary C. 2001. *Black Identities: West Indian Immigrant Dreams and American Realities.* Cambridge, MA: Harvard University Press.

Weeks, John R., Rubén G. Rumbaut, and Norma Ojeda. 1999. "Reproductive Outcomes among Mexico-Born Women in San Diego and Tijuana: Testing the Migration Selectivity Hypothesis." *Journal of Immigrant Health* 1:77-90.

Willis, Paul E. 1977. *Learning to Labour: How Working Class Kids get Working Class Jobs.* Farnborough, Eng.: Saxon House.

Wilson, William J. 1990. *The Truly Disadvantaged: The Inner City, The Underclass, and Public Policy.* Chicago: University of Chicago Press.

Zborowski, Mark and Elizabeth Herzog. 1962. *Life is with People; The Culture of the Shtetl.* New York: Schocken Books.

Zeng, Zhen and Yu Xie. 2004. "Asian-Americans' Earnings Disadvantage Reexamined: The Role of Place of Education." *American Journal of Sociology* 109:1075-1108.

Zhou, Min. 1997. "Growing up American: The Challenge Confronting Immigrant Children and Children of Immigrants." *Annual Review of Sociology* 23:63-95.

—. 1999. "Ethnicity as Social Capital: Social Support and Control in Ethnic Institutions and Immigrant Families."Pp.1-43

—. 1999. "Segmented Assimilation: Issues, Controversies, and Recent Research on the New Second Generation." Pp. 196-211 in *The Handbook of International Migration*, edited by C. Hirschman, P. Kasinitz, and J. DeWind. New York: Russell Sage Foundation.

—. 2001. "Progress, Decline, Stagnation? The New Second Generation Comes of Age." Pp. 272-307 in *Strangers at the Gates: New Immigrants in Urban America*, edited by R. Waldinger. London: University of California Press.

Zhou, Min and Carl L. Bankston. 1994. "Social Capital and the Adaptation of the Second Generation: the Case of Vietnamese Youth in New Orleans." *International Migration Review* 28:821-845.

—. 1998. *Growing up American: How Vietnamese Children adapt to Life in the United States*. New York: Russell Sage Foundation.

Index